THE *Savior* WAS BORN

A 7-Lesson Family-Style Bible
Study of the Birth of Jesus

Driven By
Grace

Lindsey Carroll

ISBN: 9798846837485

First Edition

For more resources:
Follow on Instagram @DrivenByGrace
Shop drivenbygrace.com

Table of Contents

Merry Christmas!

I'm so grateful you have chosen to use this study for your Christmas season. My goal with this study was to provide depth, context, and cultural understanding to a familiar story we may skim over because we know it so well. There is so much to learn every time we study scripture. I pray you walk away from this study with a deeper understanding and appreciation for the birth of our Savior.

I've designed this study for families with children as well as an adult Bible study. There is a commentary section that provides further context for the daily Bible reading. The commentary can also be used as a read-aloud with your kids. At the end of each lesson, I've included one page for family review and two pages for an adult Bible study. I have also provided hymns to read or sing, and crafts/recipes to do as a family.

My hope is that you and your kids can be learning scripture together. The knowledge you gain during your personal study time can be shared with your kids for fruitful discussions.

This study can be done over seven days, so you can easily complete this study during the Christmas season. Although, my prayer is that we aren't merely "fitting" God's word into our day; rather, it's our sole focus and priority. I pray we all slow down and prioritize the right things this holiday season, such as reading God's word together and worshiping our Savior!

Wishing you a blessed, safe, and healthy Christmas! May God use this study to draw you and your family closer to Him this season!

Warmest wishes,

Lindsey

The Carroll Family

Supply List

Lesson 1

Stained Glass Angel Ornament

- [ ] Tissue Paper
- [ ] Watercolor Paint
- [ ] Paint Brushes
- [ ] Cardstock
- [ ] Glue Stick
- [ ] Twine
- [ ] Laminator & Sheets

Lesson 2

O Little Town of Bethlehem Ornament

- [ ] Tree Slice
- [ ] Sheet Music to Bethlehem Song (pg. 96)
- [ ] Matte Mod Podge + Brush
- [ ] Twine
- [ ] Pencil & Sharpie
- [ ] Eye Hook

Lesson 3

Graham Cracker Manger & Nativity

- [ ] Graham Crackers
- [ ] Frosting or Hot Glue
- [ ] Shredded Coconut
- [ ] Gumdrops
- [ ] Pretzel Sticks
- [ ] Animal Crackers
- [ ] Toothpicks

Lesson 4

Peppermint Hot Chocolate

- [ ] Milk (any kind)
- [ ] Cocoa or Cacao Powder
- [ ] Maple Syrup
- [ ] Pure Peppermint Extract
- [ ] Pure Vanilla Extract
- [ ] Optional: Whipped Cream + Candy Canes

Lesson 5

Gold, Frankincense & Myrrh Playdough

- [ ] All-Purpose Flour
- [ ] Cream of Tartar
- [ ] Frankincense Essential Oil
- [ ] Myrrh Essential Oil
- [ ] Olive Oil
- [ ] Yellow Food Coloring
- [ ] Gold Glitter
- [ ] Salt

Lesson 6

Egyptian Butter Cookies

- [ ] Ghee (clarified butter)
- [ ] Powdered Sugar
- [ ] All-Purpose Flour
- [ ] Piping Bag
- [ ] Optional: Sliced Almonds or Pistachios

Lesson 7

Cinnamon Stick Cross Ornament

- [ ] Cinnamon Sticks
- [ ] Hot Glue
- [ ] Red and White Twine
- [ ] Scissors

Cinnamon Apple Cider

- [ ] Cinnamon Sticks
- [ ] 12 Gala or Fuji Apples
- [ ] 2 Green Apples
- [ ] Whole Cloves
- [ ] Ginger
- [ ] Salt
- [ ] Brown Sugar or Maple Syrup

Read-Aloud Suggestions

If you are looking for Christmas picture books to add to your home library, then these are great options to check out! You can buy these books with the links below (Amazon affiliate links), or check online used book stores like Thrift Books and Better World Books. I also saved all the read-aloud versions on a YouTube Playlist. There are many ways to enjoy these beautiful picture books!

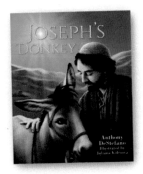

Joseph's Donkey by Anthony DeStefano
A sweet story of a donkey, whose great purpose was to carry Mary to Bethlehem and watch Jesus grow into a man.

The Legend of the Candy Cane by Lori Walburg
Explains the Christian symbolism behind the candy cane and how it relates to Jesus. Read this book with the suggested activity for Lesson 4.

Little Star by Anthony DeStefano
A tale of the meaning behind the star on a Christmas tree. This book makes the connection of the star being a reminder that the wise men followed the star to Bethlehem.

The First Christmas Night by Keith Christopher
A rhyming story that retells the story of Jesus' birth.

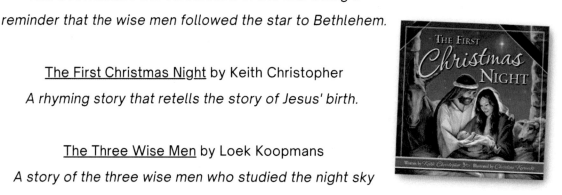

The Three Wise Men by Loek Koopmans
A story of the three wise men who studied the night sky and decided to follow a star to find the newborn King.

The Little Shepherd's Christmas by Carol Heyer
A sweet story of a shepherd boy who worked in the field and was able to see the Savior of the world be born.

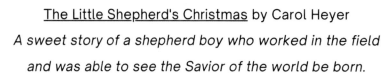

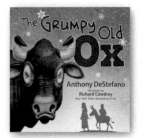

The Grumpy Old Ox by Anthony DeStefano
A grumpy, blind ox meets Jesus and his life is changed.

<u>The Christmas Miracle of Jonathan Toomey</u>
by Susan Wojciechowski
A heartwarming story of a woodcarver whose cold heart is changed after helping a little boy recreate his lost nativity scene. This book has also been made into a movie.

<u>Humphrey's First Christmas</u> by Carol Heyer
A cute and funny tale of a camel who meets Jesus. A sweet, lighthearted book with great illustrations.

<u>The Good News of Christmas</u> by Rousseaux Brasseur
This Christmas book will be a staple in my house! It's all rhyming and tells an accurate, biblical story of the birth of Jesus.

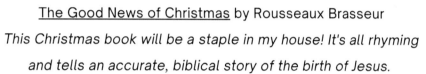

<u>Mary's First Christmas</u> by Walter Wangerin Jr.
A beautiful book of Mary telling young Jesus the story of His birth. Very endearing and helps show the humanity of Jesus and what it may have been like for Him growing up.

<u>The Christmas Story</u> by Carol Heyer
This book tells the most complete Christmas story from both gospel accounts. This older version also accurately shows the wise men meeting Jesus later in His childhood.

<u>The Newborn King</u> by Pat Thompson
A biblically accurate telling of the birth of Jesus by using scripture from Luke 2.

<u>Tonight You Are My Baby</u> by Jeannine Norris
This book sweetly shares Mary's perspective of loving Jesus as her child first before the world meets Him.

	LESSON 1	LESSON 2	LESSON 3
TOPIC:	Gabriel Announces God's Plan to Mary	Journey to Bethlehem	The Birth of Jesus Christ
BIBLE:	Luke 1:26-56	Luke 2:1-5 Matthew 1:18-25	Luke 2:6-21
LISTEN TO PODCAST:	Nativity Dramatization Podcast ep. 1	Nativity Dramatization Podcast ep. 2	Nativity Dramatization Podcast ep. 3
HYMNS:	O Come, O Come, Immanuel	O Little Town of Bethlehem	The Shepherd Watchers
CRAFTS & RECIPES:	Stained Glass Angel Ornament	O Little Town of Bethlehem Ornament	Graham Cracker Nativity

Podcast Note: The podcast I am recommending for this study is an absolute joy to listen to! The creators of the podcast made the story of Jesus' birth come to life with over 60 actors, an orchestra, background noises, and the hustle and bustle of what it would have been like for Mary and Joseph in the Holy Land. It truly is a "movie for your mind." I hope you take the time to play the episodes for yourself and your kids this Christmas. Each episode is about 30 minutes long. I'm sure it will become a holiday favorite!

LESSON 4	LESSON 5	LESSON 6	LESSON 7
Jesus Presented at the Temple	The Wise Men & King Herod	Flight to Egypt	Return to Nazareth
Luke 2:22-38	Matthew 2:1-11	Matthew 2:12-18	Matthew 2:19-23 Luke 2:39-40
Nativity Dramatization Podcast ep. 4	Nativity Dramatization Podcast ep. 5		
Joyful, Joyful, We Adore Thee	When From The East The Wise Men Came What Star Is This, With Beams So Bright	Why, Herod, Unrelenting Foe	Childhood of Jesus Christmas Carol (From Heaven Above to Earth I Come)
Peppermint Hot Chocolate	Gold, Frankincense, and Myrrh Playdough	Egyptian Butter Cookies	Cinnamon Stick Cross Cinnamon Apple Cider

NAZARETH, ISRAEL

GABRIEL ANNOUNCES GOD'S PLAN TO MARY

LUKE 1:30-31 ESV

And the angel said to her, "Do not be afraid, Mary, for you have found favor with God. And behold, you will conceive in your womb and bear a son, and you shall call his name Jesus.

Pray and Then read...

Birth of Jesus Foretold

26 In the sixth month the angel Gabriel was sent from God to a city of Galilee named Nazareth,

27 to a virgin betrothed to a man whose name was Joseph, of the house of David. And the virgin's

name was Mary. 28 And he came to her and said, "Greetings, O favored one, the Lord is with you!"

29 But she was greatly troubled at the saying, and tried to discern what sort of greeting this might

be. 30 And the angel said to her, "Do not be afraid, Mary, for you have found favor with God.

31 And behold, you will conceive in your womb and bear a son, and you shall call his name Jesus.

32 He will be great and will be called the Son of the Most High. And the Lord God will give to him

the throne of his father David, 33 and he will reign over the house of Jacob forever, and of his

kingdom there will be no end."

34 And Mary said to the angel, "How will this be, since I am a virgin?"

35 And the angel answered her, "The Holy Spirit will come upon you, and the power of the Most

High will overshadow you; therefore the child to be born will be called holy—the Son of God.

36 And behold, your relative Elizabeth in her old age has also conceived a son, and this is the sixth

month with her who was called barren. 37 For nothing will be impossible with God." 38 And Mary

said, "Behold, I am the servant of the Lord; let it be to me according to your word." And the angel

departed from her.

Mary Visits Elizabeth

39 In those days Mary arose and went with haste into the hill country, to a town in Judah,

40 and she entered the house of Zechariah and greeted Elizabeth. 41 And when Elizabeth heard

the greeting of Mary, the baby leaped in her womb. And Elizabeth was filled with the Holy Spirit,

42 and she exclaimed with a loud cry, "Blessed are you among women, and blessed is the fruit of

your womb! 43 And why is this granted to me that the mother of my Lord should come to me?

44 For behold, when the sound of your greeting came to my ears, the baby in my womb leaped for

joy. 45 And blessed is she who believed that there would be a fulfillment of what was spoken to

her from the Lord."

Mary's Song of Praise: The Magnificat

46 And Mary said,

"My soul magnifies the Lord,

47 and my spirit rejoices in God my Savior,

48 for he has looked on the humble estate of his servant.

For behold, from now on all generations will call me blessed;

49 for he who is mighty has done great things for me,

and holy is his name.

50 And his mercy is for those who fear him

from generation to generation.

51 He has shown strength with his arm;

he has scattered the proud in the thoughts of their hearts;

52 he has brought down the mighty from their thrones

and exalted those of humble estate;

53 he has filled the hungry with good things,

and the rich he has sent away empty.

54 He has helped his servant Israel,

in remembrance of his mercy,

55 as he spoke to our fathers,

to Abraham and to his offspring forever."

56 And Mary remained with her about three months and returned to her home.

Gabriel Announces God's Plan to Mary

In the story of Jesus' birth, a prominent angel named Gabriel was responsible for delivering God's divine message to the people. First, Gabriel visited a priest named Zechariah and told him that he and his wife, Elizabeth, would have a baby boy in their old age. Six months after delivering that message, Gabriel visited Mary and told her she would become pregnant with God's Son by the Holy Spirit.

Mary was a virgin— a young woman who was pure and unmarried. She is believed to have been between the ages of 12 and 16 years old. In the ancient Jewish culture, it was not uncommon for women to be engaged for marriage at the age of 12 and have children by 14 or 16 years old. Although it seems young to us today, it was not odd back then; it was expected.

Men and women married in their teens to begin having a family early in life to ensure their family name would carry on with many descendants. Parents arranged marriages for their sons and daughters with other families. In their culture, it was not Mary's age that would have shocked the people; it would have been her pregnancy without being properly married to Joesph.

Although Mary was young, she was very mature in her faith. Gabriel revealed to Mary that she had found favor in God's eyes and was chosen to be the mother of the Messiah. He revealed that she would become pregnant supernaturally by the Holy Spirit and give birth to a baby boy that was both human and God.

At the time of Gabriel's announcement, Mary was betrothed to Joseph, meaning they were legally bound to be married. In ancient Jewish culture, there were three stages to a marriage: engagement, betrothal, and marriage.

Engagement: A formal agreement made by the fathers to arrange a marriage between their daughter and son.

Betrothal: The groom's father would pay the bride's father a bride-price of 50 shekels or more (Exod. 22:16-17, Deut. 22:28-29). Paying the bride-price made the engagement legally binding and would begin the betrothal period. If either of them decided to cancel the betrothal, it would be equivalent to a divorce.

Marriage: After the bride-price was paid, the groom would return home to his father's house and prepare the bridal chamber. This is where he and his bride would live. This could take up to a year or more to prepare. The bride always left her father's household to become part of the groom's family. That was why having sons was important in their culture because it allowed their families to grow larger. The groom's father would determine when the bridal chamber was finished and would send the groom to get his bride. During that waiting period, the bride would be preparing and eagerly waiting for her groom. The groom would return unexpectedly for his bride to begin their wedding feast, which would last about one week. The bride would bring a dowry to the marriage given by her father. The dowry was either money, clothes, household goods, servants, or whatever else would help the couple begin their life together successfully.

After Mary received the news that she would become pregnant with the Savior, she left Nazareth and traveled to the hill country of Judea to visit her cousin Elizabeth. When she arrived, Elizabeth was six months pregnant after experiencing a life of barrenness. The Lord miraculously helped Elizabeth and Zechariah have their first child in their old age. The journey to Elizabeth's home could have taken 3-5 days. Mary was a young girl, so this trip to Elizabeth's home was courageous. She most likely traveled in a caravan group to stay protected from bandits on the road.

When Mary arrived and greeted Elizabeth, the six-month-old baby inside Elizabeth's womb (John the Baptist) was filled with the Holy Spirit and leaped for joy. It is so amazing to see this detail explained in scripture. The Holy Spirit was moving in the life of an unborn child while in its mother's womb. Mary stayed with Elizabeth for the first three months of her pregnancy and then returned home to Nazareth.

Gabriel

Gabriel is an angel who stands in the presence of God (Luke 1:19). In the Old Testament, God sent Gabriel to visit Daniel to interpret his prophetic dreams (Dan. 8:15-27, Dan. 9:20-27). In the book of Daniel, we are told that Gabriel had the appearance of a man. He is also the angel who revealed to Zechariah that he and his wife, Elizabeth, would have a baby named John the Baptist. Lastly, Gabriel is the angel who announced to Mary that she would carry God's Son, Jesus. All those who encountered Gabriel were initially filled with fear, but he reassured them not to fear him.

Mary

Mary was a young woman, assumed to be between 12-16 years old, and betrothed to be married to Joseph. Mary was a godly woman who rightfully feared the Lord. She became pregnant through supernatural means by the Holy Spirit. Mary was obedient to the Lord and faithful to her husband. She raised Jesus, the Messiah, as well as additional sons and daughters from her marriage with Joseph (Luke 8:19). She became a widow by the time Jesus reached adulthood and began His public ministry. When Jesus died, He asked His disciple, John, to take care of her— a responsibility Jesus would have had as her eldest son.

Elizabeth

Elizabeth was the wife of a priest named Zechariah and a relative to Mary. She was old and beyond childbearing years when she became pregnant with her first child, John the Baptist. This was a miraculous pregnancy that defied nature. Elizabeth is the mother of John the Baptist, the prophet who prepared the way for Jesus. John shared a message of repentance and pointed everyone to the Messiah.

Nazareth

Mary lived in a small town called Nazareth, in the region of Galilee. The town of Nazareth is located 15 miles from the Sea of Galilee. Nazareth did not have a good water supply, just a small well in the middle of the village. It's believed at the time of Jesus' birth, that only about 200-500 people lived in the city. It was a very small and insignificant town to the Jewish people. The people of Nazareth would have been fishermen or farmers— specifically producing wine, olive oil, wheat, and barley.

Family Review

Comprehension Questions:

1. What is the name of the angel who revealed God's plan to Mary? *Gabriel*
2. What message did Gabriel reveal to Mary? *That she would carry God's Son.*
3. Did Mary doubt the angel or did she believe? *She had faith and believed.*
4. How did Mary become pregnant? *Through the power of the Holy Spirit.*
5. Whom did Mary visit after receiving her life-changing news? *Her relative, Elizabeth.*
6. What was the difference between engagement and betrothal in ancient Jewish culture? *The engagement wasn't legally binding. A betrothal was a contract to be married that could only be broken by divorce.*
7. What happened when Mary greeted Elizabeth? *Elizabeth's baby leaped for joy in her womb.*
8. Who was Elizabeth pregnant with? *John the Baptist*

Application Questions:

1. What surprised you the most about the process for marriage in the ancient Jewish culture?
2. How would you respond if God revealed a plan for your life that was the opposite of what you were expecting? How can you prepare to surrender to the Lord's plans over your own?
3. Although Mary was young, the Lord was able to use her in the most mighty of ways. How can you let the Lord use you for His glory and purpose at a young age?
4. Mary was likely judged and gossiped about by others for her unique situation. How do you think Mary stayed focused on the Lord's plan for her life vs. caring what others thought about her? How can you do the same?

Key Bible Verse:

"And the angel said to her, "Do not be afraid, Mary, for you have found favor with God. And behold, you will conceive in your womb and bear a son, and you shall call his name Jesus."
Luke 1:30-31

Family Prayer:

Heavenly Father,

Thank you for the Bible that you have written for us to learn about you and your amazing story. We ask for you to help us center our hearts and minds on you and not ourselves this season. Help us be obedient to your word and willing to surrender our lives to your will. We know your purpose and plans are better than our own. We trust you and love you. In Jesus' name, Amen.

1. Luke 1:27 emphasizes that Mary was betrothed to Joseph, a man from the house of David. Read 2 Samuel 7:12-16 where the prophet, Nathan, spoke to King David about the Lord's promise for his kingdom and descendants. What did God promise King David?

_____

_____

_____

2. Mary and Joseph were both from the bloodline of King David. Although Jesus was not Joseph's biological Son, He was his legally adopted Son and, therefore, a legal heir to the throne of King David. The Lord's promise to David was partially fulfilled through his son, Solomon, but how was it ultimately fulfilled through God's Son, Jesus? Read Luke 1:32-33.

_____

_____

_____

3. Mary became pregnant through the power of the Holy Spirit. Jesus received a physical body like men, but inherited His eternal, sinless nature from the Holy Spirit. Why is it important that Jesus was not conceived through Joseph's seed? Read Romans 5:12-14 to understand the root of sin nature.

_____

_____

_____

4. Jesus' birth was a fulfillment of many Old Testament prophecies. Read these verses and note what they say so you can keep them top of mind as you study Jesus' birth in the coming lessons. I've also provided the estimated years before Jesus' birth that these prophecies were written.

Genesis 3:15 *(1,400 yrs)* _____

Numbers 24:17 *(1,400 yrs)* _____

Isaiah 7:14 *(700 yrs)* _____

Isaiah 9:6-7 *(700 yrs)* _____

Hosea 11:1 *(750 yrs)* _____

5. After reading these prophecies and seeing how many years prior to Jesus' birth they were promised by the Lord, what does this reveal about God?

_____

_____

_____

_____

Reflect

1. Mary's life plans were changed in a single moment. The life she thought she was going to have was completely altered after encountering the angel, Gabriel. What moments in your life have altered the course you were on? How can you see God's faithfulness through your situations?

_____

_____

_____

2. Write down the words Mary spoke after receiving the life-altering news for her life. (Luke 1:38)

_____

_____

_____

3. Is there an area in your life where you are struggling to surrender and say, "_I am your servant, let it be to me according to your word?_" How can you change your attitude in difficult circumstances to be rooted in humility and trust in the Lord?

_____

_____

_____

4. What aspect of God's character do you understand more clearly after reading today's passage? What does this truth of God mean for your walk as a Christian?

_____

_____

_____

Pray

_____

_____

_____

_____

_____

Hymn

O Come, O Come, Immanuel
Written by John Mason Neale (1851)

1 O come, O come, Immanuel,
and ransom captive Israel
that mourns in lonely exile here
until the Son of God appear.

Rejoice! Rejoice! Immanuel
shall come to you, O Israel.

2 O come, O Wisdom from on high,
who ordered all things mightily;
to us the path of knowledge show
and teach us in its ways to go.

Rejoice! Rejoice! Immanuel
shall come to you, O Israel.

3 O come, O come, great Lord of might,
who to your tribes on Sinai's height
in ancient times did give the law
in cloud and majesty and awe.

Rejoice! Rejoice! Immanuel
shall come to you, O Israel.

4 O come, O Branch of Jesse's stem,
unto your own and rescue them!
From depths of hell your people save,
and give them victory o'er the grave.

Rejoice! Rejoice! Immanuel
shall come to you, O Israel.

5 O come, O Key of David, come
and open wide our heavenly home.
Make safe for us the heavenward road
and bar the way to death's abode.

Rejoice! Rejoice! Immanuel
shall come to you, O Israel.

6 O come, O Bright and Morning Star,
and bring us comfort from afar!
Dispel the shadows of the night
and turn our darkness into light.

Rejoice! Rejoice! Immanuel
shall come to you, O Israel.

7 O come, O King of nations, bind
in one the hearts of all mankind.
Bid all our sad divisions cease
and be yourself our King of Peace.

Rejoice! Rejoice! Immanuel
shall come to you, O Israel.

Stained Glass Angel Ornament

Supplies:

- Tissue paper
- Watercolor paints
- Paint brushes
- Cardstock
- Glue stick
- Twine
- Laminator
- Laminating sheets

Directions:

1. Fold the cardstock in half (hamburger style) and draw half of the outline of an angel, with the center of the body at the crease of the fold. Cut out the angel.

2. Cut out parts of the angel so the tissue paper can show through. To make it easier, fold the areas you want to cut before trimming like the wings, head, and lower part of the body.

3. Paint different patterns on a piece of tissue paper with your watercolor paint. Only slightly wet the brush so you don't drench the tissue paper. Add stripes, swirls, or polka dots for fun patterns.

4. Place your angel outline on top of your tissue paper, and trim the excess paper so they match in size. You can also tear small portions of tissue paper and glue over the different openings for more colors and textures.

5. Apply glue on the border of the angel and apply the tissue paper pieces.

6. Once glued, you can add any extra decorations to the angel like painting the white border with glitter glue.

7. After the angel is dry, laminate and cut it out to make it sturdy.

8. Punch a hole at the top and string with twine to hang on your tree or somewhere in your home.

Craft idea inspired by: Artcampla.com

LESSON 2

JOURNEY TO BETHLEHEM

LUKE 2:1 ESV

In those days a decree went out from Caesar Augustus that all the world should be registered.

Pray and Then read...

The Birth of Jesus Christ

1 In those days a decree went out from Caesar Augustus that all the world should be registered.

2 This was the first registration when Quirinius was governor of Syria. 3 And all went to be registered, each to his own town. 4 And Joseph also went up from Galilee, from the town of Nazareth, to Judea, to the city of David, which is called Bethlehem, because he was of the house and lineage of David, 5 to be registered with Mary, his betrothed, who was with child.

Matthew 1:18-25

The Birth of Jesus Christ

18 Now the birth of Jesus Christ took place in this way. When his mother Mary had been betrothed to Joseph, before they came together she was found to be with child from the Holy Spirit. 19 And her husband Joseph, being a just man and unwilling to put her to shame, resolved to divorce her quietly. 20 But as he considered these things, behold, an angel of the Lord appeared to him in a dream, saying, "Joseph, son of David, do not fear to take Mary as your wife, for that which is conceived in her is from the Holy Spirit. 21 She will bear a son, and you shall call his name Jesus, for he will save his people from their sins." 22 All this took place to fulfill what the Lord had spoken by the prophet:

23 "Behold, the virgin shall conceive and bear a son,
  and they shall call his name Immanuel" (which means, God with us).

24 When Joseph woke from sleep, he did as the angel of the Lord commanded him: he took his wife, 25 but knew her not until she had given birth to a son. And he called his name Jesus.

Journey to Bethlehem

When Mary returned home from visiting Elizabeth, she, at some point, revealed the news to Joseph that she was pregnant. Because they were betrothed to be married and were in a legally binding relationship, Joseph had the right to divorce Mary, or worse, have her stoned to death for breaking their betrothal by supposedly committing adultery. However, the Bible tells us that Joseph was a just man, and he made plans to leave her quietly to avoid publicly shaming her.

After Joseph planned to leave Mary quietly, an angel spoke to him in a dream. The angel revealed that Mary was, in fact, pregnant by the Holy Spirit, and the baby was the long-awaited Messiah. Joseph believed the angel and immediately obeyed God by taking Mary as his wife. Joseph committed to remain faithful to Mary and help raise Jesus as his adopted Son.

Both Mary and Joseph were descendants of King David. Joseph was from the royal bloodline through David's son, King Solomon, and Mary was from David's son Nathan. God made a covenant with King David that his kingdom would be established and reign forever (2 Sam. 7:11-16). This forever kingdom was only made possible through the birth of the Messiah. The fact that both Mary and Joseph were from the line of David was an important fulfillment of prophecy. When Jesus was born, He was called the Son of David because of His lineage. Joseph was Jesus' earthly adoptive father, making Jesus a legal heir to the throne of David.

Before Jesus was born, Caesar Augustus (the first emperor of Rome) issued a decree for a census to be taken of the land. The census was a way for Rome, the world leader, to properly count the people living in the land so they could collect taxes. Caesar Augustus required everyone to travel back to their ancestral hometowns to register for taxation. There weren't TVs or phones back then to hear about the decree, so a Roman centurion would have traveled to the cities to deliver the message. Since Joseph was originally from Bethlehem, the city of David, he and Mary had to leave Nazareth to travel there to register for the census.

The journey from Nazareth to Bethlehem was about 80-90 miles. This journey would have taken about 4-5 days of travel by foot, but possibly longer for someone who was pregnant— up to 10 days. Mary and Joseph would have traveled on a caravan route, planning their trip around water wells for refreshment for themselves and a donkey if they had one. The route they walked would have been desert terrain that was lined with olive trees in some areas. The beginning of the journey would have been easier as it was flat terrain, but it would have become increasingly more difficult as they got closer to Bethlehem, which was situated on a hill.

The important thing about this story is to remember that God is in control. God can use world leaders to bring His prophecies and plans to fulfillment. God used Caesar Augustus to issue a decree that would require Mary and Joseph to travel to Bethlehem. Micah 5:1-5 prophesied that a great ruler would be born from that little town 700 years before Jesus was born. God is in control of all things, and through the birth story of Jesus, we see how God used a world leader to bring His ultimate good plan to fruition.

PROPHECY WRITTEN OVER 700 YEARS BEFORE JESUS WAS BORN:

2 But you, O Bethlehem Ephrathah, who are too little to be among the clans of Judah, from you shall come forth for me one who is to be ruler in Israel, whose coming forth is from of old, from ancient days. 3 Therefore he shall give them up until the time when she who is in labor has given birth; then the rest of his brothers shall return to the people of Israel. 4 And he shall stand and shepherd his flock in the strength of the Lord, in the majesty of the name of the Lord his God. And they shall dwell secure, for now he shall be great to the ends of the earth. 5 And he shall be their peace. — Micah 5:2-5

Joseph

Joseph was the man chosen by God to be the husband of Mary and the earthly, adoptive father of Jesus. Joseph was a just man who loved God, knew the scriptures (the Old Testament Law), and obeyed the Lord. He was a carpenter (Matthew 13:55) and faithfully raised Jesus according to the Law. He was a protector and provider for his family. He is a great example of humility, self-control, and obedience to the Lord. Joseph was not present at Jesus' crucifixion, so he likely died sometime before Jesus' ministry began, leaving Mary a widow.

Caesar Augustus

Caesar Augustus was the first emperor of Rome from 27 BC to 14 AD. He was the great-nephew of Julius Caesar, who adopted him as his son. He is most known for creating stability and peace in the Roman Empire, called the Pax Romana, which means Roman Peace in Latin. Under Caesar's leadership, the Romans expanded the roads throughout the regions so their military forces could travel quickly. Those roads were used by the people living in the land of Israel and allowed the spread of Christianity to happen quickly after the death of Jesus.

Bethlehem

Bethlehem is a small village on a hill and was primarily significant because it was the birthplace of King David. Bethlehem is located 6 miles south of Jerusalem, the capital city of Israel. It has a Mediterranean climate, with hot and dry summers and cold and rainy winters. There were fertile fields, orchards, and vineyards that surrounded the city. Significant things that happened in Bethlehem were: the burial site for Rachel, Ruth and Boaz's story, David's hometown and where he was anointed as king, and the birthplace of Jesus. Today, Bethlehem is considered a city in Palestine. The territory was handed over to Palestinian authorities in the 1990s and is primarily a Muslim population.

Family Review

1. What helped Joseph believe that Mary was pregnant by the Holy Spirit? *An angel spoke to him in a dream.*
2. Who issued a decree for a census to be taken of the land? *Caesar Augustus*
3. Why did Caesar Augustus want a census to be taken? *To properly tax the people*
4. Where were Mary and Joseph living when the decree was given? *Nazareth*
5. What city were they required to travel to in order to complete the census? *Bethlehem*
6. Which significant king of Israel was born in Bethlehem (besides Jesus)? *King David*
7. Which prophet wrote a prophecy about a ruler coming from the little town of Bethlehem 700 years before Jesus was born? *Micah*

Application Questions:

1. After the angel spoke to Joseph in a dream, he woke up and was immediately obedient to take Mary as his wife. How can we show immediate obedience when God commands us to do something?
2. Have you ever felt led to do something from the Holy Spirit? If yes, did you obey? If you didn't obey, how can you learn from that experience and obey the next time? (Parents: share your experiences, too!)
3. God spoke to Joseph in a dream through an angel, and He speaks to us today through His word, the Bible. How can we hear from God daily?

Key Bible Verse:

"In those days a decree went out from Caesar Augustus that all the world should be registered."
Luke 2:1

Family Prayer:

Heavenly Father,

Thank you for showing us that you are always in control. Even in the most difficult times, we know you see us and that you care about our situation. Just like with Mary and Joseph, you had a purpose and plan for them to fulfill Caesar's decree so your Son would be born in Bethlehem. Help us remember that you are in control and that we can faithfully trust in you.

In Jesus' name, Amen.

1. When Joseph first found out about Mary's pregnancy, what did he decide to do with their relationship? (Matthew 1:19)

_____

_____

_____

2. Read Deut. 22:23-24. What was the Law for a woman engaged to be married, but committed adultery with another man?

_____

_____

_____

3. Israel was chosen by God to be a holy nation that was set apart from the rest of the world. They were to live sinless lives and diligently follow the Law to be holy before God. Why was it important to deal with the sexual sin committed within the nation? Read 1 Corinthians 5 for Paul's perspective on how sexual sin impacts the body of believers.

_____

_____

_____

4. Based on the severity of the Law for sexual sin among the Israelites, how important is sexual purity to God? Why do you think God cares so much about sexual purity? Read Hebrews 13:4 and 1 Corinthians 6:18-20 to help your answer.

_____

_____

_____

5. Now that you understand the Law and penalty for sexual sin in Israel, how does that help your understanding of Joseph's initial reaction to Mary's news?

_____

_____

_____

6. What did Joseph specifically not do with Mary until after Jesus was born? (Matthew 1:25) Why do you think Joseph made that decision? What does that decision reveal about Joseph?

_____

_____

_____

1. Mary and Joseph were ordinary people chosen by God for a great purpose. The Bible shows that prior to their calling, they were both living a life of obedience to the Lord. They knew the scriptures, but more importantly, they obeyed what the scriptures said. How can you be preparing your life and heart to be used by God, so that when He calls on you, you will be ready to say yes?

2. Matthew references Isaiah 7:14, which is a prophecy about the coming Messiah. The name in the prophecy is Immanuel, which means "God with us." Jesus is God in the flesh who resurrected to heaven, but how is God still with us today? Read John 14:15-20, 1 John 4:15, and Ephesians 4:30.

3. What aspect of God's character do you understand more clearly after reading today's passage? What does this truth of God mean for your walk as a Christian?

Pray

Hymn

O Little Town of Bethlehem
Written by Phillips Brooks (1868)

1 O little town of Bethlehem,
how still we see thee lie!
Above thy deep and dreamless sleep
the silent stars go by;
yet in thy dark streets shineth
the everlasting light.
The hopes and fears of all the years
are met in thee tonight.

2 For Christ is born of Mary,
and, gathered all above
while mortals sleep, the angels keep
their watch of wond'ring love.
O morning stars, together
proclaim the holy birth,
and praises sing to God the King
and peace to all the earth.

3 How silently, how silently,
the wondrous gift is giv'n!
So God imparts to human hearts
the blessings of his heav'n.
No ear may hear his coming,
but in this world of sin,
where meek souls will receive him, still
the dear Christ enters in.

4 O holy Child of Bethlehem,
descend to us, we pray,
cast out our sin and enter in,
be born in us today.
We hear the Christmas angels
the great glad tidings tell;
O come to us, abide with us,
our Lord Immanuel!

O Little Town of Bethlehem Ornament

Supplies:

- Tree slice
- O Little Town of Bethlehem Hymn Sheet Music (see appendix pg. 96)
- Matte Mod Podge and brush
- Pencil
- Sharpie
- Twine
- Small eye hook

Directions:

1. Print out the sheet music to the song *O Little Town of Bethlehem.* You can download the music from Hymnary.org or make a copy of the sheet music provided in the appendix of this study on page 96. If you print online, I recommend shrinking the size, so the words are smaller and more lyrics can fit on the ornament.

2. Place your tree slice on top of the sheet music and trace the outline with a pencil.

3. Cut out the sheet music so it's slightly smaller than the tree slice.

4. Brush a layer of mod podge onto the tree slice and then adhere your music sheet to the tree slice—brush additional layers of mod podge on top of the sheet music.

5. Once fully dry, twist an eye hook into the top of your tree slice and string it with twine to hang. If you don't have an eye hook, you can drill a small hole through the top of your ornament and hang it with twine.

6. *Optional:* You can draw a Bethlehem town outline on top of the sheet music for an extra creative touch—color in the outline with a black marker.

Craft idea inspired by: Lovelyetc.com

SANCTAE CATHARINAE VIRGINI ET MARTIRI DICATVM

THE BIRTH OF JESUS CHRIST

LUKE 2:11-12 ESV

For unto you is born this day in the city of David a Savior, who is Christ the Lord. And this will be a sign for you: you will find a baby wrapped in swaddling cloths and lying in a manger.

Pray and Then read...

6 And while they were there, the time came for her to give birth. 7 And she gave birth to her firstborn son and wrapped him in swaddling cloths and laid him in a manger, because there was no place for them in the inn.

The Shepherds and the Angels

8 And in the same region there were shepherds out in the field, keeping watch over their flock by night. 9 And an angel of the Lord appeared to them, and the glory of the Lord shone around them, and they were filled with great fear. 10 And the angel said to them, "Fear not, for behold, I bring you good news of great joy that will be for all the people. 11 For unto you is born this day in the city of David a Savior, who is Christ the Lord. 12 And this will be a sign for you: you will find a baby wrapped in swaddling cloths and lying in a manger." 13 And suddenly there was with the angel a multitude of the heavenly host praising God and saying,

14 "Glory to God in the highest,

and on earth peace among those with whom he is pleased!"

15 When the angels went away from them into heaven, the shepherds said to one another, "Let us go over to Bethlehem and see this thing that has happened, which the Lord has made known to us." 16 And they went with haste and found Mary and Joseph, and the baby lying in a manger. 17 And when they saw it, they made known the saying that had been told them concerning this child. 18 And all who heard it wondered at what the shepherds told them. 19 But Mary treasured up all these things, pondering them in her heart. 20 And the shepherds returned, glorifying and praising God for all they had heard and seen, as it had been told them.

21 And at the end of eight days, when he was circumcised, he was called Jesus, the name given by the angel before he was conceived in the womb.

The Birth of Jesus Christ

While Mary and Joseph were in Bethlehem registering for the census, the time came for her to give birth to Jesus. The scriptures tell us Mary laid Jesus in a manger because there was no room for them in the inn. The word "inn" is the Greek word "katalyma," which means lodging place or guest room. When we read this story, we tend to think there was no room in a hotel-style lodging, but in ancient Israel, many homes had a guest-chamber for travelers. Hospitality was important in the Jewish culture, and people would offer family and strangers a place to stay while they were in town. So, there may have also been no room in a family's guest-chamber.

While we may not know the exact place Jesus was born, there are three different theories that Bible scholars speculate occurred based on scripture and Jewish culture. The first possibility (and the most popular) was that Mary and Joseph stayed in an animal stable near an inn. The second possibility was that they were offered the lower part of an Israeli home, where the animals were kept because the upper guest-chambers were filled with other guests.

The third possibility (and not as commonly known) is that Jesus may have been born in a place called the "Tower of the Flock" known as Migdal Eder. This was a lookout tower in the northern part of Bethlehem. The lower part of the tower was where the Levitical shepherds would inspect the sacrificial lambs at birth for the temple sacrifice. This tower is mentioned in Genesis 35:21 where

Rachel died and was buried, and it is also mentioned in Micah 4:8 regarding the prophecy of the restoration of Jerusalem. The tower of the flock is used figuratively to represent the royal line of David that comes from Bethlehem.

Scholars believe the shepherds in the nearby field of Bethlehem were temple shepherds. This means these were people who took care of the lambs that would be offered for the daily sacrifices at the temple. The temple shepherds would have their flock graze in the nearby fields next to the Temple of the Flock (Migdal Eder). These shepherds would have been trained experts in selecting a perfect lamb to offer as a sin offering at the temple.

Luke tells us the shepherds were watching their flock by night, which may indicate it was a season when ewes were giving birth. During birthing season, shepherds often lived among the sheep to keep track of the lambs being born. According to the Law of Moses, the firstborn unblemished male lamb belonged to the Lord as a sacrifice, so they needed to properly identify those lambs. Ewes often give birth to two or more lambs at a time, so shepherds needed to be diligent and present for each birth.

The shepherds would wrap the lambs in swaddling cloths and place them in a manger to inspect them for blemishes and protect them from injuries. If the firstborn male lamb was without blemish, illness, or defect, then he could be sacrificed to the Lord as a sin offering. Likewise, Jesus was God's firstborn Son, who was sinless (without blemish) and would grow up to be the perfect sin offering. Jesus is called the Lamb of God by John the Baptist in John 1:29.

The third theory of where Jesus was born is very interesting and may help explain how the shepherds knew exactly where to look for Jesus in Bethlehem. If the third theory is accurate, then the shepherds wouldn't have wandered through the streets of Bethlehem, but rather, would have run straight to the Temple of the Flock to look for the specific sign from the angels— a baby wrapped in cloths and lying in a manger (an animal feeding trough), just like the many sacrificial lambs prior.

The Savior of the world was born in the most humble conditions. He could have been born in a royal palace among the elite, but instead, he chose to enter the world in a humble and significant way. Once the shepherds found Jesus, they praised God for leading them to the Messiah, and they told Mary and Joseph all that the angels revealed to them. Jesus' birth was really anything but a "silent night." Jesus had the most amazing birth announcement with a host of angels praising and worshiping Him in the night sky!

Jesus

Jesus Christ is God in the flesh. God knew there was no perfect and holy sacrifice to satisfy the payment for all sins, so He chose to send His Son to be that sacrifice for all people. Jesus was born as a baby who had to be nurtured, fed, nursed, and trained. He is a human just like you and me, but He is sinless and perfect. Jesus is fully human and fully God. He faced temptations just like every person, but He overcame them through the power of the Holy Spirit. Jesus is God's chosen Son. He is part of the trinity and equal to God the Father and the Holy Spirit. Jesus is the Savior of the world, and through faith in Him only, we receive forgiveness for our sins and eternal life with God. Jesus is alive today, sitting at the right hand of God in heaven.

Shepherds

Shepherds were not respected in Israel and were considered social outcasts. People despised shepherds because they usually allowed their animals to graze in fields that belonged to others. They had low social and religious status in Israel. They were considered unreliable sources and were not allowed to testify in court. In a family, the youngest son was often the shepherd of the flock. Once the boy grew stronger, he would help his father plow and harvest crops and pass the shepherding duties down to the next youngest son. We see an example of this with David, the youngest of eight sons, who shepherded his father's flock before becoming king (1 Sam. 16:11). Shepherds had to protect the flock from predators and lead them to fresh water and food daily. Some key people who were also shepherds in the Bible include Abraham, Isaac, Jacob, Joseph, Moses, and David.

Bethlehem

Bethlehem, the city of David, is where Samuel found David as a young shepherd and anointed him as king of the Jews. It was also in Bethlehem where the shepherds found Jesus, a baby in a manger, the King of Kings, and Savior for all people.

Family Review

Comprehension Questions:

1. In what city did Mary give birth to Jesus? *Bethlehem*
2. What did Mary do with Jesus after she gave birth? *She wrapped Him in swaddling cloths and laid Him in a manger.*
3. What is a manger? *A feeding trough for animals.*
4. Who did the Lord choose to share the news of the birth of Jesus with first? *Shepherds*
5. What were the shepherds doing when they heard the news? *Keeping watch over their flock by night.*
6. Who delivered the news to the shepherds? *The angel of the Lord.*
7. How would the shepherds know when they found the baby, the Messiah? *He would be wrapped in swaddling cloths and lying in a manger.*

Application Questions:

1. If Jesus had been born in a home or palace, how would that have made it difficult for the shepherds to find Him?
2. God doesn't care about popularity, fame, social status, or wealth. Instead, God cares about our hearts and willingness to serve and obey Him. Is there something you are pursuing and prioritizing more than your obedience to God?
3. The shepherds had the job of sharing the good news with everyone they saw to let them know the Savior had been born. We also have a responsibility to share the good news that the Savior died for our sins and rose again. Who is one person you could share this good news with? Pray together as a family for an opportunity to reach that person.

Key Bible Verse:

"For unto you is born this day in the city of David a Savior, who is Christ the Lord."
Luke 2:11

Family Prayer:

Heavenly Father,

Thank you for sending your Son to be born as a baby in Bethlehem. Thank you for that good news, and the good news that Jesus died for our sins so we could be forgiven by you. Thank you for sending Jesus to the world to provide a way for salvation for us. Help us seek the lost and confidently share the good news of the gospel with them this season. We love you and praise you. In Jesus' name, Amen.

Study

1. When the angel of the Lord told the shepherds that the Savior was born, who did the angel say the good news was for? (Luke 2:10) Why is this important?

_____

_____

_____

_____

2. The angel listed three titles for baby Jesus—Savior, Christ, and Lord (Luke 2:11). Let's define each of those titles with scripture.

Savior: Read Matthew 1:21, John 3:16-18, and Romans 3:23

_____

_____

_____

Christ (also means Messiah): Read Luke 4:17-21, John 4:25-26, John 20:31, and Acts 10:39-43

_____

_____

_____

Lord (title of authority; Jesus is God): Read John 1:1-3, John 13:13, Acts 2:36-38, and Philippians 2:9-11

_____

_____

_____

3. Read Galatians 4:4-7. Summarize the significance of Jesus' birth based on Paul's explanation.

_____

_____

_____

4. Shepherds were not considered a reliable source in ancient Israel. Their testimony was often disregarded and they were looked down upon. Why do you think God would share His amazing news with shepherds first instead of the elite or religious leaders?

_____

_____

_____

Reflect

1. The shepherds were told of the birth of Jesus, and through faith, they sought Jesus in Bethlehem. After finding Him, they proclaimed the good news to all. How can you be like the shepherds by intentionally seeking Jesus daily and sharing His good news of salvation with all?

2. Read John 10:1-18. Jesus calls Himself the "Good Shepherd." How is Jesus like a shepherd? Think about the duties of a shepherd as well as the social status of that time.

3. Read Matthew 28:19-20. We have been given a command by Jesus to share the good news with others and make disciples. How can you fulfill this command within your home? How can you fulfill this command with others outside your home?

4. What aspect of God's character do you understand more clearly after reading today's passage? What does this truth of God mean for your walk as a Christian?

Pray

Hymn

The Shepherd Watchers
Written by Nahum Tate (1600-1700s)

1 While humble shepherds watched their flocks
in Bethlehem's plains by night,
an angel sent from heaven appeared,
and filled the plains with light.

2 'Fear not' he said, for sudden dread
had seized their troubled mind;
'Glad tidings of great joy I bring
to you and all mankind.

3 'To you in David's town, this day,
is born, of David's line,
the Saviour, who is Christ the Lord;
and this shall be the sign:

4 'The heavenly Babe you there shall find
to human view displayed,
all meanly wrapped in swathing-bands,
and in a manger laid.'

5 Thus spake the seraph; and forthwith
appeared a shining throng
of angels praising God; and thus
addressed their joyful song:

6 'All glory be to God on high,
and to the earth be peace;
good will is shown by heaven to men
and never more shall cease.'

Graham Cracker Nativity Scene

Supplies:

- Graham crackers
- Frosting
- Gumdrops
- Toothpicks
- Pretzel sticks
- Animal crackers
- Shredded coconut (toasted)
- *Optional: Hot glue*

Tip: If you don't care about eating the nativity scene after you make it, then I recommend using hot glue instead of frosting to help make it sturdy. I used hot glue for this picture.

Directions:

For the manger:

1. Break a graham cracker piece in half the short way, so you have two square crackers. One of these will be the base for your manger.
2. Break one of the square pieces in half so you have two small pieces to build the manger.
3. Place a strip of frosting (or hot glue) on the base cracker.
4. Stick your two smaller graham cracker pieces on top of the frosting/glue in a v-shape.

For the nativity scene:

1. Spread shredded coconut on a baking sheet and broil for 2 min. Keep an eye on the coconut so it doesn't burn. You just want it slightly toasted. Set aside.
2. Grab five graham crackers to build a two-tiered stable. Assemble the **bottom half** with one long rectangle graham cracker and two halves for the side walls. Adhere with frosting or hot glue. Assemble the **top half** with two long rectangle graham crackers and two halves for the side walls. Assemble both levels together with frosting or hot glue.
3. **Mary, Joseph, shepherds, and the angel:** stick three gumdrops on a toothpick or hot glue three candies together. For the angel, cut a gumdrop in half and glue the pieces to the back for wings. **Baby Jesus**: stick two gumdrops on a toothpick or glue them together.
4. Place the manger in the stable, sprinkle with hay (coconut), and add baby Jesus.
5. Give each shepherd a pretzel stick for their staff.
6. Sprinkle the scene with toasted coconut to represent the hay and add the animal crackers.

Craft idea inspired by: Gluesticksblog.com

JERUSALEM, ISRAEL

LESSON 4

JESUS PRESENTED AT THE TEMPLE

LUKE 2:22 ESV

And when the time came for their purification according to the Law of Moses, they brought him up to Jerusalem to present him to the Lord.

Pray and then read...

Luke 2:22-38

Jesus Presented at the Temple

22 And when the time came for their purification according to the Law of Moses, they brought him up to Jerusalem to present him to the Lord 23 (as it is written in the Law of the Lord, "Every male who first opens the womb shall be called holy to the Lord") 24 and to offer a sacrifice according to what is said in the Law of the Lord, "a pair of turtledoves, or two young pigeons." 25 Now there was a man in Jerusalem, whose name was Simeon, and this man was righteous and devout, waiting for the consolation of Israel, and the Holy Spirit was upon him. 26 And it had been revealed to him by the Holy Spirit that he would not see death before he had seen the Lord's Christ. 27 And he came in the Spirit into the temple, and when the parents brought in the child Jesus, to do for him according to the custom of the Law, 28 he took him up in his arms and blessed God and said,

29 "Lord, now you are letting your servant depart in peace,

   according to your word;

30 for my eyes have seen your salvation

31   that you have prepared in the presence of all peoples,

32 a light for revelation to the Gentiles,

   and for glory to your people Israel."

33 And his father and his mother marveled at what was said about him. 34 And Simeon blessed them and said to Mary his mother, "Behold, this child is appointed for the fall and rising of many in Israel, and for a sign that is opposed 35 (and a sword will pierce through your own soul also), so that thoughts from many hearts may be revealed."

36 And there was a prophetess, Anna, the daughter of Phanuel, of the tribe of Asher. She was advanced in years, having lived with her husband seven years from when she was a virgin, 37 and then as a widow until she was eighty-four. She did not depart from the temple, worshiping with fasting and prayer night and day. 38 And coming up at that very hour she began to give thanks to God and to speak of him to all who were waiting for the redemption of Jerusalem.

49

Jesus Presented at the Temple

Mary and Joseph were obedient to the Law of Moses and careful to follow all of the Lord's commandments. Forty days after Jesus was born, Mary and Joseph went to Jerusalem to fulfill the purification laws for childbirth and to present Jesus to the Lord. In Leviticus 12, the Lord gave specific instructions for women after they had a baby. For a son, the boy had to be circumcised at eight days old, and then 33 days later, the mother had to offer a burnt offering and a sin offering to the Lord. All firstborn males belonged to God and had to be redeemed before the Lord per the Old Covenant (Exodus 34).

According to the Law, they were supposed to bring a lamb for a burnt offering and a pigeon for a sin offering. However, if they couldn't afford a lamb, they could offer two turtledoves or two pigeons instead. Luke tells us that Mary offered two birds, which is an indication that they were likely poor.

When Mary and Joseph went to the temple in Jerusalem, they encountered a man named Simeon. We don't know much about this man other than the fact that he was a righteous and devout Jew. The Holy Spirit revealed to Simeon that he would not die without seeing the Lord's Christ. The title Christ comes from the Greek word "Christos" which means Messiah — deliverer, Savior, and anointed one from the line of King David.

Through the prompting of the Holy Spirit, Simeon went to the temple the same day that Mary and Joseph arrived to fulfill the purification law. When Simeon saw Jesus, who was only a 6-week-old infant, he knew He was the Lord's Messiah. Simeon took Jesus into his arms and blessed God for sending the Savior to the world. He thanked God for fulfilling His promise of letting him see the Savior before he died.

Simeon made an interesting statement when he said his blessing at the temple— that Jesus would be the Savior for the Gentiles *and* the Jews. Gentile is a word that means a person who is not a Jew — other nations and people groups. For hundreds of years, the Jews were eagerly awaiting for their Messiah to come and rescue them from their enemies and oppressors; similar to how God used Moses to save the Jewish people from their slavery in Egypt. Simeon prophesied that Jesus came to save the Gentiles and the Jews. Jesus would save them both by delivering them from the bondage of sin and providing a way for forgiveness to enter the Lord's presence. The birth of Jesus was amazing news for all people — Jew and Gentile.

Simeon also prophesied to Mary that the birth of her child would lead to great sorrow. Many people would not believe in Jesus as the Messiah, leading to a great fall and rising of Israel. Simeon told Mary that a sword would pierce her soul, meaning she would experience great heartache for her child. Of course, Mary did experience that terrible heartache over 30 years later when she watched her Son be crucified on a cross.

There was a second person that Mary and Joseph encountered at the temple that day; a prophetess named Anna. A prophetess was a female prophet — someone who received messages from God to share with others. Anna was an old woman who married at a young age, but lived as a widow for the majority of her life. She was a devout Jew who didn't remarry after her husband of seven years died. Instead, she spent most of her time at the temple worshiping, praying, fasting, and prophesying. When Anna saw the infant Jesus, she immediately knew He was the Savior and proclaimed it to all who were there in Jerusalem.

In God's sovereignty and full knowledge, He purposefully chose Mary and Joseph to be Jesus' earthly parents. They not only fulfilled prophecy by being from the line of David and by having a virgin conception, but they were also obedient Jews who kept God's commandments and taught them to His Son. From eight days old, Mary and Joseph made sure to follow the Lord's commands and do all that was written in the Law of Moses. God chose obedient parents, who would raise Jesus in a God-centered home. Jesus was without sin His whole life and fulfilled the Law perfectly— from infancy to adulthood. God intentionally placed Jesus in a family that would love Him well by obeying scripture.

Simeon

Simeon was a righteous and devout Jew. The Holy Spirit revealed to Simeon that he would not die until he saw the Messiah with his own eyes. He followed the prompting of the Holy Spirit and went to the temple at the same time that Mary and Joseph went to offer their purification sacrifices. Simeon held 6-week-old baby Jesus in his arms and prophesied that Jesus was the long-awaited Messiah who would save the Israelites and Gentiles. After seeing Jesus with his own eyes, he was filled with peace because the Lord fulfilled His promise.

Anna

Anna is one of the few women in the Bible who is called a prophetess— a female prophet. A prophet in the Bible is someone who spoke directly to God to share His words and messages with others. Anna married her husband at a young age, but they were only married for seven years before he died. After his death, she remained a widow and dedicated her life to the service of the Lord. Other prophetesses in the Bible include Deborah, Miriam, and Huldah.

Jerusalem

Jerusalem is the capital city of Israel, where the Jewish temple was once located. The city has been completely destroyed twice— in 586 BC and 70 AD. The city is located on top of a limestone plateau in the Judean mountains, 35 miles east of the Mediterranean Sea. Jerusalem has warm, dry summers and cool, rainy winters. The Jewish people were required to travel to Jerusalem three times a year to be present for three Jewish feasts. Jerusalem was a very important city during Jesus' time and still is today. Today, Jerusalem has three main religions: Christianity, Islam, and Judaism. The Muslim mosque is located where the Jewish temple once existed.

Family Review

Comprehension Questions:

1. In what city did Mary and Joseph offer their purification sacrifices? *Jerusalem*
2. What animal did Mary and Joseph offer to the Lord for their sacrifice? *Two birds*
3. What did Mary's sacrifice reveal about the wealth of her and Joseph? *They didn't have enough money to buy a lamb, so they were allowed to offer the sacrifice of the poor.*
4. Who did the Lord promise would see the Messiah before he died? *Simeon*
5. What did Simeon do when he saw baby Jesus? *He held Him in his arms and thanked the Lord for seeing the Messiah.*
6. Who else saw Jesus and knew He was the Messiah? *The female prophetess, Anna.*
7. What do we know about Anna? *That she was a widow for many years and served the Lord.*

Application Questions:

1. Simeon and Anna were old in their age, but never lost faith in the Lord to fulfill His promise of providing a Savior for Israel. Have you ever doubted God's faithfulness? What can you think about to remember that God is true and always faithful in keeping His promises?
2. The Lord doesn't care about the amount of money or offerings brought to Him; He cares about the heart behind the gift. Read 2 Corinthians 9:6-7 and discuss what it means to be a cheerful giver.
3. Tell of a time when you blessed someone. How did it make you feel? Who can you bless this Christmas?

Key Bible Verse:

"And when the time came for their purification according to the Law of Moses, they brought him up to Jerusalem to present him to the Lord."
Luke 2:22

Family Prayer:

Heavenly Father,

Thank you for your Word and for allowing us to read our Bible every day to learn about you. We pray our hearts are centered on you this season and every day. Please open our eyes to see those in need that we can bless. We pray we have hearts that desire to serve you all of our days like Simeon and Anna. Help us be obedient to your Word. We love you and we praise you.

In Jesus' name, Amen.

1. Read Leviticus 12:1-8 to understand the offerings required per the Law of Moses that Mary and Joseph were obeying in this part of the story. Write down the commands for a male child specifically.

A woman was unclean for how many days? _____

What occured on the 8th day? _____

A woman was unclean for how many more days? _____

After the woman was clean, what did she bring to the priest at the tabernacle (temple in Jesus' day):

Burnt offering: _____   Sin offering: _____

If the woman was poor, what was she allowed to bring in place of a lamb?

Burnt offering: _____   Sin offering: _____

2. What did Mary and Joseph do after the birth of Jesus to obey the Mosaic Law?

Luke 2:21 _____

Luke 2:22-24 _____

3. Why was it important for Jesus to be born into a family that prioritized obedience to the scriptures?

_____

_____

_____

_____

4. God has given us instructions on how to raise our children just like He did for Mary and Joseph. Read these scriptures and write down how God wants us to raise our children.

Deuteronomy 6:5-7 _____

Proverbs 22:6 _____

Psalm 127:3-5 _____

Ephesians 6:4 _____

5. The Law of Moses states that the testimony of two or more people is needed to confirm an event actually took place (Deut. 19:15). How did Simeon and Anna play an important role as eyewitnesses to Jesus' fulfillment of the Law?

_____

_____

_____

_____

Reflect

1. Children are a blessing from the Lord and should be raised to know Him, their Creator. How are you raising your children to know and obey God's commands?

2. How are you modeling **obedience** to the Lord's word and commands for your children to see? Write down what you are doing well.

3. How are you modeling **disobedience** to the Lord's word and commands for your children to see? Write down what you need to improve and pray over these things.

4. What aspect of God's character do you understand more clearly after reading today's passage? What does this truth of God mean for your walk as a Christian?

Pray

Hymn

Joyful, Joyful, We Adore Thee
Written by Henry Van Dyke (1907)

1 Joyful, joyful, we adore You,

God of glory, Lord of love;

Hearts unfold like flow'rs before You,

Op'ning to the sun above.

Melt the clouds of sin and sadness;

Drive the dark of doubt away;

Giver of immortal gladness,

Fill us with the light of day!

2 All Your works with joy surround You,

Earth and heav'n reflect Your rays,

Stars and angels sing around You,

Center of unbroken praise;

Field and forest, vale and mountain,

Flow'ry meadow, flashing sea,

Chanting bird and flowing fountain

Praising You eternally!

3 Always giving and forgiving,

Ever blessing, ever blest,

Well-spring of the joy of living,

Ocean-depth of happy rest!

Loving Father, Christ our Brother,

Let Your light upon us shine;

Teach us how to love each other,

Lift us to the joy divine.

4 Mortals, join the mighty chorus,

Which the morning stars began;

God's own love is reigning o'er us,

Joining people hand in hand.

Ever singing, march we onward,

Victors in the midst of strife;

Joyful music leads us sunward

In the triumph song of life.

Healthy Peppermint Hot Chocolate

Supplies:

- 2 cups milk (your milk preference)
- 2 Tbsp cocoa or cacao powder
- 3 Tbsp maple syrup
- ½ tsp pure vanilla extract
- ⅛ tsp pure peppermint extract
- Pinch of salt
- Optional toppings: whipped cream and crushed candy cane pieces

Directions:

1. Add milk, cocoa powder, maple syrup, vanilla extract, peppermint extract, and salt to a saucepan.
2. Whisk over medium heat until everything is melted and well combined. Taste and add more syrup if you desire it sweeter.
3. Pour into mugs and top with whipped cream and crushed candy cane pieces if desired.

Optional:

Enjoy your peppermint hot chocolate while reading or listening to the book _The Legend of the Candy Cane_ by Lori Walburg. It's a sweet story of a candy maker who explains the important meaning of the candy cane by connecting the shape and colors to Jesus. I have the read-aloud version saved on my YouTube playlist for this study.

"J" Shape
J for Jesus
Same shape as a shepherd's staff

Red Color
Jesus' blood shed for our sins

White Color
Jesus cleanses our sins and makes us white as snow

Striped Pattern
By His stripes we are healed (Isaiah 53:5 NKJV)

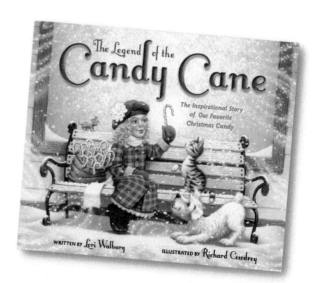

GATES OF ALL NATIONS
IN PERSEPOLIS, IRAN
(ANCIENT PERSIA)

LESSON 5

THE WISE MEN & KING HEROD

MATTHEW 2:1-2 ESV

Now after Jesus was born in Bethlehem of
Judea in the days of Herod the king, behold,
wise men from the east came to Jerusalem,
saying, "Where is he who has been born
king of the Jews? For we saw his star when
it rose and have come to worship him."

Pray and then read...

The Visit of the Wise Men

1 Now after Jesus was born in Bethlehem of Judea in the days of Herod the king, behold, wise men from the east came to Jerusalem, 2 saying, "Where is he who has been born king of the Jews? For we saw his star when it rose and have come to worship him." 3 When Herod the king heard this, he was troubled, and all Jerusalem with him; 4 and assembling all the chief priests and scribes of the people, he inquired of them where the Christ was to be born. 5 They told him, "In Bethlehem of Judea, for so it is written by the prophet:

6 "'And you, O Bethlehem, in the land of Judah,
   are by no means least among the rulers of Judah;
for from you shall come a ruler
   who will shepherd my people Israel.'"

7 Then Herod summoned the wise men secretly and ascertained from them what time the star had appeared. 8 And he sent them to Bethlehem, saying, "Go and search diligently for the child, and when you have found him, bring me word, that I too may come and worship him." 9 After listening to the king, they went on their way. And behold, the star that they had seen when it rose went before them until it came to rest over the place where the child was. 10 When they saw the star, they rejoiced exceedingly with great joy. 11 And going into the house, they saw the child with Mary his mother, and they fell down and worshiped him. Then, opening their treasures, they offered him gifts, gold and frankincense and myrrh.

The Wise Men & King Herod

The gospel of Luke shares the details of Jesus' birth, while the gospel of Matthew shares the details of what occurred after Jesus' birth. Unlike popular tradition, the wise men (magi) were not present for the birth of Jesus. The wise men actually met Jesus several months to possibly two years after He was born. They had traveled far from the East, likely from Persia or Babylon, which was an 800-mile trip or more. This journey would have taken them at least 4 months.

The Bible also doesn't specifically tell us how many wise men visited Jesus. Tradition states there were three men based on the number of gifts brought to Jesus. However, based on the commotion and attention they received when they arrived in Jerusalem, it's possible that it was a larger number of people who traveled together to worship the new King of the Jews.

At that time, Herod the Great was the appointed king of the Jews by the Romans. Herod was a paranoid and evil man, always afraid of losing his power. At one time in his life, he even killed his wife and children for fear of them taking over his dynasty. His paranoia worsened towards the end of his life when he became sick.

When Herod heard there was a claim of a new king, he inquired with the experts of the scriptures, the chief priests and scribes, to understand what the prophets said about the Messiah. The religious leaders explained to Herod that Micah (a prophet in the Old Testament) wrote that the Messiah would be born in Bethlehem (Micah 5:2). The religious leaders knew the prophecy, yet they didn't bother to seek this new King themselves. They were only six miles away from their long-awaited Messiah, but instead, it was Gentile wise men who traveled over 800 miles to worship the Lord, the King of the Jews.

After the news spread throughout Jerusalem, Herod summoned the wise men secretly to find out when they first saw the Lord's star appear. He asked them to look for the new King so he could also worship Him. Of course, Herod was not being sincere. He did not really want to worship the new King of the Jews; he just wanted to know where the Child lived so that he could kill Him.

When the wise men left Herod's palace, the star reappeared and helped lead them directly to Jesus' home. When the wise men arrived at the house, they fell to their knees to worship the Child and offered Him three gifts— gold, frankincense, and myrrh. In the East, it was custom to bring some type of gift when you entered the presence of royalty. Because the wise men believed Jesus to be the Messiah, they brought lavish gifts to honor Him as a King. These gifts have significant symbolic meaning, but they were also very practical for the young family who unknowingly would have to leave their home in Bethlehem and flee to Egypt to escape Herod's evil plan.

Meaning of The Three Gifts:

Gold: Royalty

In the Bible, gold represents royalty and God's divinity. This gift was symbolic of Jesus being King and God. Important elements in the Bible that were made of gold were the ark of the covenant and all the elements inside the Tabernacle/Temple.

Frankincense: High Priest & Deity

Frankincense is an aromatic gum resin that is obtained from trees in Africa. Frankincense is used in perfumes and incense. In Exodus, God gave a specific recipe of spices to use for offering incense in the Holy Place, and frankincense was one of the spices (Exodus 30:34-38). The priests would burn the incense inside the Lord's temple as a pleasing aroma to the Lord. This gift represented Jesus as our High Priest and offering Himself as a perfect and pleasing sacrifice to the Lord.

Myrrh: Suffering

Myrrh was a spice from trees used for medicine, cosmetics, and embalming. When Jesus was on the cross, the Roman soldiers offered Him wine mixed with myrrh as a type of medicine to numb the pain. When Jesus was buried, He was wrapped in cloths and anointed with oil and myrrh. The gift of myrrh was symbolic of the suffering and affliction Jesus would endure in His life up to the cross.

Wise Men

The wise men, also called magi, were astronomers and astrologers from the East. In ancient culture, magi studied the movement of the planets and stars as a way to interpret divine messages for their religion. Being from the East, they were probably from Arabia, Persia, or Babylon and an advisor to a king in one of those areas. These men were likely affluent based on the lavish gifts they brought to Jesus. Scholars believe the wise men were Gentile people who traveled a long distance to find the Messiah. They fully expected the Jewish people to be praising the newborn King of the Jews, only to discover they didn't even know He had been born. The wise men gave their time, treasures, and worship to the Lord.

King Herod (Herod the Great)

Herod was the king of Judea when Jesus was born. Herod was a descendant of Esau, Jacob's brother, and therefore an Edomite. He was made king of the Jews by the Romans, but did not practice the Jewish Law. Herod initially ruled as governor of Galilee in 41 BC, but had favor with the Romans and was appointed as king of Judea. To take his title as king of Judea, he had to fight the Hasmonean dynasty, who ruled Judea at that time. After three years of fighting, he defeated the dynasty and became king of Judea from 37/36 BC to 4 BC.

Herod is known for renovating the Lord's temple to make it bigger and grander than the first. He is also remembered for his cruel acts of murder during his reign. Herod constantly feared losing power and control of Judea. This led him to kill his own family members, including his wife and sons, because they were part of the Hasmonean dynasty— the rival dynasty. Herod died in 4 BC from a severe illness in the land of Jericho.

The East

In the Bible, the East is often associated with people outside the nation of Israel. In the story of the wise men, scholars believe they came from the land of Persia, Arabia, or Babylon. These areas were known for their wealth and were located 800+ miles away. The journey would have been a long, hard, and dangerous journey, especially because of the expensive gifts they were carrying. That is why it's believed they traveled with a large caravan group for protection from thieves and robbers.

Family Review

Comprehension Questions:

1. Where did the wise men travel from? *The East*
2. Who was the king of Judea when Jesus was born? *King Herod (Herod the Great)*
3. What did King Herod ask the wise men to do? *To find the baby that was being called the King of the Jews and report back to him with His location.*
4. Which prophet wrote about the Messiah being born in Bethlehem? *Micah*
5. Where did the wise men find Jesus? *In a house with Mary.*
6. What did the wise men do when they saw Jesus? *They worshiped Him and offered Him gifts.*
7. What gifts did the wise men offer Jesus? *Gold, frankincense, and myrrh*

Application Questions:

1. The wise men were persistent and determined to find the Savior. They never gave up despite the difficulties they may have faced. How can you be encouraged to keep seeking Jesus when times get hard? What is something hard you are facing that you should not give up on?
2. What types of things can be a distraction from worshiping God during Christmas? What can you do this Christmas season to make it a priority to seek Jesus?
3. If Jesus came to your house this Christmas, would He feel like He is being worshiped as King? If not, what changes can you make to worship Jesus, the King of Kings, this Christmas?

Key Bible Verse:

"Now after Jesus was born in Bethlehem of Judea in the days of Herod the king, behold, wise men from the east came to Jerusalem, saying, 'Where is he who has been born king of the Jews? For we saw his star when it rose and have come to worship him.'"
Matthew 2:1-2

Family Prayer:

Heavenly Father,

Thank you for sending your Son to be born in this world so we could be saved. We pray that you will help us focus on worshiping and praising you. Help us focus on giving you gifts of our time, worship, and treasures instead of focusing on what *we will* receive this season. We have already received the greatest gift of all from you— the free gift of salvation through your Son, Jesus. Help us stay focused on you. Use us to bring you glory, Lord. We love you and praise you.

In Jesus' name, Amen.

1. The wise men traveled far from the East because they saw the King's star in the sky. They viewed it as a sign of a newborn Jewish King. Read Numbers 24:17, and write down the significance of this prophecy in relation to the birth of Jesus.

2. The wise men studied the sky for signs and predictions from the stars and planets. This practice was actually condemned by the Lord in the Old Testament. How does the story of the wise men show God reaching out to the Gentile people and leading them to the ultimate source of Truth?

3. How could the wise men have known about the Jewish prophecies? Read Daniel 2:46-49 to see the power and influence Daniel had in Babylon after he and the Jewish people were exiled from their land. Also, read Daniel 9:20-26 and note which angel revealed to Daniel the meaning of his prophecy regarding the Messiah.

4. King Herod was a violent man, known for rage and killing people to keep his power. He became very angry when he heard there was another person being given the title "King of the Jews." Matthew 2:3 also states that *all Jerusalem* was troubled with him. Why do you think the people living in Jerusalem would have been troubled by this news given to Herod?

5. Read Matthew 2 and write down the different responses these people had to the birth of Christ:

King Herod:

Scribes:

Wise men:

Reflect

1. The religious leaders and scribes knew the scriptures and prophecies written about the birth of the Messiah, yet they didn't seek Him. How can you make sure you aren't puffed up with knowledge, yet lacking love for Christ?

2. The Lord met the wise men where they were in their field of study. He graciously led them on a long journey to find the Truth. Reflect on your journey and relationship with Christ. How has God been gracious to you by leading you to His Truth?

3. The wise men had faith that the star they saw was a sign of the coming Messiah. They believed the prophecies and made a long journey based solely on faith. Read Hebrews 11:1 and 11:6. Write of a time when you obeyed God in faith.

4. What aspect of God's character do you understand more clearly after reading today's passage? What does this truth of God mean for your walk as a Christian?

Pray

Hymns

When From The East The Wise Men Came
Written by John Henry Hopkins (1892)

1 When from the East the wise men came,
Led by the Star of Bethlehem,
The gifts they bro't to Jesus were
Of gold, and frankincense, and myrrh.

2 Bright gold of Ophir, passing fine,
Proclaims a King of royal line;
For David's son in David's town,
Is born the heir of David's crown.

3 The incense-clouds, with fragrance rare,
The presence of a God declare;
Lo! kings in adoration fall,
For Mary's son is Lord of all.

4 The myrrh, with bitter taste, foreshows
A life of sorrows, wounds and woes;--
The deadly cup, that overran
With anguish for the Son of Man.

5 Our gold upon Thine altar lies;
Our prayers to Thee, as incense, rise;
Accept as myrrh our tears and sighs:
O King, O God, O Sacrifice!

Amen.

What Star Is This, With Beams So Bright
Written by Charles Coffin (1736)

1 What star is this, with beams so bright,
More lovely than the noonday light?
'Tis sent to announce a newborn king,
Glad tidings of our God to bring.

2 'Tis now fulfilled what God decreed,
"From Jacob shall a star proceed;"
And lo! the eastern sages stand
To read in heav'n the Lord's command.

3 O Jesus, while the star of grace
Impels us on to seek thy face,
Let not our slothful hearts refuse
The guidance of thy light to use.

4 To God the Father, heav'nly Light,
To Christ, revealed in earthly night,
To God the Holy Spirit raise
An endless song of thankful praise!

Source: Hymnary.org

Gold, Frankincense, & Myrrh Playdough

Supplies:
- 1 cup all-purpose flour
- ¼ cup salt
- 2 tsp cream of tartar
- 1 cup water
- 2 Tbsp olive oil
- 10 drops of Frankincense essential oil *(more or less depending on how strong you want the smell)*
- 10 drops of Myrrh essential oil *(more or less depending on how strong you want the smell)*
- 4 drops of yellow food coloring
- Gold glitter

Directions:
1. Combine all the dry ingredients into an unheated saucepan and stir to combine.
2. Add yellow food coloring to the 1 cup of water. Stir and pour into the pan. Then, add the olive oil and essential oils and stir to combine.
3. Turn your stove to medium heat and stir constantly with a wooden spoon until it combines into a ball. It should thicken fairly quickly (3-5 minutes).
4. Once the mixture becomes one big ball, remove it from the heat and knead until it is smooth.
5. Place the playdough in a bowl and sprinkle with glitter. Mix well until all the glitter is folded into the dough. Play and enjoy! Store in an air-tight container for up to 3 months.

Discuss the significance of the ingredients as you make the playdough:
- **Salt:** Salt was used as a preservative and a disinfectant in Israel. It was required to season all grain offerings with salt that were brought to the Lord. The Dead Sea was a key source of salt for Israel.
- **Olive Oil:** Olive oil was used to light lamps, anoint kings, and sanctify the priests and all the elements inside the tabernacle. Olive oil was a sign of richness and health. It was also symbolic of the Holy Spirit.
- **Frankincense:** Frankincense is a very fragrant scent used to make perfumes and incense. It was burned continuously inside the tabernacle as a pleasing aroma to God (Exodus 30:34-38). It was also used as a healing oil.
- **Myrrh:** Myrrh was a perfume and an embalming oil. It was the oil applied to Jesus' body when He died. Jesus was offered wine mixed with myrrh on the cross to lessen the pain, but Jesus denied the drink. (Mark 15:23, John 19:38-40)
- **Gold:** Gold was a precious metal in ancient Israel. Gold was symbolic of God's purity and holiness. All the elements inside the temple and tabernacle were covered in gold.

FLIGHT TO EGYPT

MATTHEW 2:13 ESV

Now when they had departed, behold, an angel of the Lord appeared to Joseph in a dream and said, "Rise, take the child and his mother, and flee to Egypt, and remain there until I tell you, for Herod is about to search for the child, to destroy him."

Blank for double-sided printing

Pray and Then read...

12 And being warned in a dream not to return to Herod, they departed to their own country by another way.

The Flight to Egypt

13 Now when they had departed, behold, an angel of the Lord appeared to Joseph in a dream and said, "Rise, take the child and his mother, and flee to Egypt, and remain there until I tell you, for Herod is about to search for the child, to destroy him." 14 And he rose and took the child and his mother by night and departed to Egypt 15 and remained there until the death of Herod. This was to fulfill what the Lord had spoken by the prophet, "Out of Egypt I called my son."

Herod Kills the Children

16 Then Herod, when he saw that he had been tricked by the wise men, became furious, and he sent and killed all the male children in Bethlehem and in all that region who were two years old or under, according to the time that he had ascertained from the wise men. 17 Then was fulfilled what was spoken by the prophet Jeremiah:

18 "A voice was heard in Ramah,

weeping and loud lamentation,

Rachel weeping for her children;

she refused to be comforted, because they are no more."

Flight to Egypt

After the wise men presented their gifts to Jesus, the Lord gave them a warning in a dream. God revealed to the wise men that Herod had an evil plan and would use their information of Jesus' location to kill Him. Therefore, God warned them not to pass through Jerusalem on their way home, so they could avoid King Herod and not report back to him.

The wise men were obedient and took a much longer route home to protect the Messiah and obey the Lord's directions. Because they were likely with a larger entourage of people, they could not pass through any main roads in Jerusalem without being noticed. Therefore, scholars believe they probably journeyed south and then up towards Gaza, which is located near the coast of the Mediterranean Sea. The direct route from their country to Jerusalem was already a long journey, but they were willing to extend this trip to obey the Lord's commands.

When Herod discovered that the wise men had deceived him, he became enraged. Herod had a history of killing people to keep his power and authority in Judea. As we learned in the previous lesson, Herod even killed his wife and sons out of his paranoia to keep his power as king. He was a terrible ruler and someone that directly showed Satan's opposition to Jesus.

Herod used the wise men's information about when they first saw the star as a way to determine what age of children to kill. This helps us know that the wise men may have presented their gifts to Jesus when he was around two years old because Herod killed all baby boys who were two years old and younger. It was a terrible act and a time of deep sorrow and anguish for the Jewish people. Innocent babies were killed because of a sinful man's jealousy, anger, and greed for power.

Bethlehem was a small city, estimated to have about 300 people living there at the time Jesus was born. Scholars speculate that this means Herod would have killed approximately 12-20 babies based on the population ratio. Regardless of the number, any innocent child killed is a terrible act of violence, and the Lord will rightfully judge Herod one day.

Through that time, we see how the Lord was sovereign and protected the life of Jesus. In the middle of the night, God spoke to Joseph in a dream and warned him to flee to Egypt to escape Herod's evil plan. Joseph is a great example of what it looks like to obey the Lord immediately. Joseph did not delay by getting a few extra hours of sleep. Instead, he woke his wife and sleeping Child in the middle of the night, packed their things, and left their home in the dark to head to Egypt. The border of Egypt from Bethlehem was about 100 miles away. This was not an easy journey, but one that needed to be made in order to protect his wife and Child.

The wise men's gifts were likely a source of income for Joseph and Mary's journey. The Lord miraculously provided for their needs because He knew in advance that they would need income for their journey to Egypt. If we can learn anything from Mary and Joseph, it is that the Lord cares for His people. We also learn that following the Lord's plans does not guarantee an easy life. Mary and Joseph experienced many hardships like the cultural shame for Mary being pregnant before marriage, their Son's birth in an animal stable, and having to flee to a new country when Jesus was about two years old. However, through their hardships, they never lost faith in the Lord. They remained obedient to God's commands because they knew He was good and that they could trust His plans for their life.

Joseph and Mary traveled to Egypt to seek refuge from Herod. Egypt was a Roman province and was outside of Herod's jurisdiction, so they would have found safety there. There was a well-established Jewish community that lived in Egypt, so it made sense for Mary and Joseph to travel there. They remained in Egypt until Herod died, which could have been anywhere from six months to several years.

King Herod (Herod the Great)

Herod's goal in life was to leave a legacy of success and power with his architectural achievements such as his palace, the Herodium, expansions to the second Jewish temple, water supplies for Jerusalem, and many more. However, all of his architectural buildings have been destroyed, and he is left with a legacy of being a tyrant, evil king, and murderer. During Herod's life, he murdered many people including 300 prominent leaders, his brother-in-law during a polo game, one of his ten wives, three sons, and the two-year-old baby boys during Jesus' childhood. When Herod was nearing his death, he was very paranoid that no one would mourn his death, and rightfully so, since he was an evil man. Therefore, he ordered prominent Jewish men to be taken to Jericho to be killed once he died to ensure there would be some type of mourning at his death. Thankfully, according to historical accounts, his final wish was not fulfilled.

Egypt

During the Greco-Roman period, many Jewish people built communities in Egypt, particularly around the city of Alexandria near the coast of the Mediterranean Sea. Egypt became under Rome's rule in 30 BC when Ceasar Augustus became the first emperor of Rome. Jews were respected in Egypt, and it was a safe place for Mary and Joseph to live during the remaining reign of King Herod in Judea. Joseph and Mary's journey from Bethlehem to Egypt may have taken five to seven days.

Family Review

Comprehension Questions:

1. How did the wise men know not to return to King Herod? *God spoke to them in a dream.*
2. What did the wise men do after the Lord spoke to them in a dream? *They went home on a different route to avoid King Herod.*
3. How did Herod respond when he found out the wise men disobeyed his orders? *He became angry and commanded all babies two years old and younger to be killed.*
4. How did God speak to Joseph? *In a dream.*
5. What did God tell Joseph? *That Herod was trying to kill baby Jesus and they needed to travel to Egypt quickly.*
6. What did Joseph do after receiving a message from God? *He rose while it was still night and took Mary and Jesus to Egypt.*

Application Questions:

1. Joseph and Mary's circumstances could have caused them to live in fear, but instead, they chose to live by faith and trust in God. What is something you are afraid of that you can surrender to God and trust in Him?
2. God is sovereign, which means He has supreme power and authority over all His creation. God was able to protect Jesus from King Herod because God knows all things before they even happen. How does it make you feel knowing God is in full control?
3. The wise men and Joseph obeyed the Lord immediately. What is one thing you can do today to practice being obedient to the Lord?

Key Bible Verse:

"Now when they had departed, behold, an angel of the Lord appeared to Joseph in a dream and said, 'Rise, take the child and his mother, and flee to Egypt, and remain there until I tell you, for Herod is about to search for the child, to destroy him.'"

Matthew 2:13

Family Prayer:

Heavenly Father,

We praise you for your sovereignty and ultimate control over all the world you created. Thank you for watching over our family and caring about every detail of our lives. Thank you for watching over Mary and Joseph so you could protect your Son, our Savior. Lord, we pray that we would trust in you and remember that you are in complete control of every situation. Thank you for loving us and protecting us. We love you. In Jesus' name, Amen.

1. How did the Lord protect Jesus from Herod? (Matthew 2:12-15) How did the wise men's obedience help Joseph?

2. When Joseph received the command from God, what details did he know? What details did he not know? (Matthew 2:13-14)

3. What applications can you draw from the few details in verse 14 regarding Mary's obedience, submission, and trust in her husband to lead their family?

4. What could have been the consequence and result if the wise men or Joseph had chosen to delay in their obedience to the Lord? What does this teach you about the importance of immediate obedience?

5. What did Herod command to happen in the region of Bethlehem? How did he determine the age of children, and what does this possibly tell us about the age of Jesus at this part of the story? (Matthew 1:7 & 2:16)

6. The wise men disobeyed King Herod, a governing authority, only when it put them at risk of being disobedient to the Lord. Likewise, we are commanded to obey and respect governing authorities unless the commands would cause us to disobey the Lord. How have you seen this lesson applicable to your life?

Reflect

1. The wise men's journey was one of **sacrifice, faith, worship,** and **obedience**. Reflect on your journey with Christ and write down your experience with God in these areas.

Journey of **sacrifice**: _____

Journey of **faith**: _____

Journey of **worship**: _____

Journey of **obedience**: _____

2. The wise men and Joseph's immediate obedience to the Lord's command saved the life of Jesus. Write of a time when your obedience to God directly impacted the life of another, or when someone else's obedience to God directly impacted your life.

_____

_____

_____

_____

3. Joseph obeyed the Lord immediately, even though he didn't have all the details. He didn't know where he would live, what he would do for work, or even how long he had to stay. He had to wait and rely on God to guide his life. How can you apply Joseph's example of obedience to your life when you are called by God and don't have all the details?

_____

_____

_____

4. What aspect of God's character do you understand more clearly after reading today's passage? What does this truth of God mean for your walk as a Christian?

_____

_____

_____

_____

Pray

_____

_____

_____

_____

_____

Hymn

Why, Herod, Unrelenting Foe
Written by Martin Luther (1500s)

1 Why, Herod, unrelenting foe!

Doth Christ the Lord's birth move thee so?

He doth no earthly kingdom crave;

Who unto us heav'n's kingdom gave.

2 The star before the wise men goes,

This light to them the true Light shows;

They, by the three gifts which they bring,

Declare this Child: God, Man, and King.

3 He was baptized in Jordan's flood,

The holy, heavenly Lamb of God,

And He, who did no sin, thereby

Cleansed us from all iniquity!

4 And now a miracle is done:

Six water pots are there of stone,

Christ speaks the word with power divine--

The water changes into wine.

5 All honor, praise to Thee be paid,

O Christ, born of the virgin maid,

With Father and with Holy Ghost,

Till time in endless time be lost.

Egyptian Butter Cookies

This is a traditional cookie you would find in Egypt called Ghorayebah. While these are simple, with only three ingredients, they require specific instructions for success. Bake these while reflecting on the lesson from today where Jesus and His family had to flee to Egypt to avoid King Herod's evil plan.

Supplies: (Makes 72 cookies - cut in half or quarter for less)

- 4 cups (500g) all-purpose flour, sifted
- 1 ½ cups (175g) powdered sugar, sifted
- 1 ⅓ cup plus 1 Tbsp (300g) ghee (in solid state— chill if needed, cannot be melted)
- Piping bag
- Optional: Sliced almonds or pistachios for topping

Tip: If you have a food scale, I highly recommend using the weighted measurements for this recipe.

Directions:

1. Sift flour and powdered sugar and place in the bowl of a stand mixer. Using the paddle attachment, blend the ingredients together.
2. Add the chilled ghee (cannot be melted), and blend on low for 5 minutes (set a timer). Increase speed to medium-high for another 5 minutes. Then, reduce speed back down to low, and blend for the last 5 minutes. Your dough should be mixed for 15 minutes total. It should be smooth, have no lumps, and resemble cake batter. This dough is *very sticky*. Do not be tempted to add more flour.
3. Scoop your batter into a piping bag.
4. Cut a large opening at the end of the bag and pipe your cookies on a prepared baking sheet with parchment paper or a silicone mat. Cookies should be 3-4 cm wide.
5. Place the cookie sheet in the fridge for 5 minutes so your dough can firm up a little and is no longer sticky. You don't want your dough to harden, so keep checking it.
6. When no longer sticky, gently press down any peaks. Make a thumbprint on each cookie and if desired add a pistachio or almond sliver on top.
7. Place the cookie sheet on the middle rack in your oven at 250° F. Bake for 17-20 minutes. You want the cookies to cook through, but remain a pale white color— they should not turn golden.
8. Once finished, let them completely cool to room temperature before touching them. If you touch them while warm, they will fall apart. If desired, sprinkle with powdered sugar on top and enjoy!

RETURN TO NAZARETH

LUKE 2:39-40 ESV

And when they had performed everything according to the Law of the Lord, they returned into Galilee, to their own town of Nazareth. And the child grew and became strong, filled with wisdom. And the favor of God was upon him.

Pray and Then read...

Matthew 2:19-23

The Return to Nazareth

19 But when Herod died, behold, an angel of the Lord appeared in a dream to Joseph in Egypt,

20 saying, "Rise, take the child and his mother and go to the land of Israel, for those who sought

the child's life are dead." 21 And he rose and took the child and his mother and went to the land of

Israel. 22 But when he heard that Archelaus was reigning over Judea in place of his father Herod,

he was afraid to go there, and being warned in a dream he withdrew to the district of Galilee.

23 And he went and lived in a city called Nazareth, so that what was spoken by the prophets might

be fulfilled, that he would be called a Nazarene.

Luke 2:39-40

The Return to Nazareth

39 And when they had performed everything according to the Law of the Lord, they returned into

Galilee, to their own town of Nazareth. 40 And the child grew and became strong, filled with

wisdom. And the favor of God was upon him.

Return to Nazareth

If you are familiar with the book of Exodus, then you will see many similarities between the life of Moses and Jesus. When Moses was born, Pharaoh commanded all the two-year-old Hebrew boys to be killed, but Moses' life was spared by his mother's protection. Likewise, Herod commanded all two-year-old boys in Bethlehem to be killed, but Jesus was spared because of His parents' obedience to flee. Moses found refuge in Egypt in Pharoah's palace, and Jesus found refuge within Egypt's borders. The Lord called Moses to lead the Israelites out of Egypt to the Promised Land, and likewise, Jesus was called out of Egypt to return to Israel when it was safe after Herod's death. These similarities were a foreshadowing of what Jesus would accomplish in His life.

Once Herod died, the Lord spoke to Joseph in another dream to provide direction for his family. The angel of the Lord told Joseph that King Herod had died, and it was now safe to return to the land of Israel. The angel didn't tell Joseph exactly where to travel, he just told him to head to Israel, and the Lord would continue to lead him. We don't know exactly how long Jesus and His family lived in Egypt; it may have been only a couple of months or a few years. The gift of gold from the wise men would have helped pay for their travels and stay. The Lord provided for their needs before they even knew they needed it.

As they traveled back to Israel, Joseph learned that Archelaus (ar-kee-lay-us), one of Herod's sons, became ruler over Judea, where the capital, Jerusalem, and the temple were located. He was afraid to settle there because Archelaus was just as evil as his father, Herod. Perhaps while traveling, Joseph got word about the massacre Archelaus caused in the temple courts right after Herod's death during Passover in 4 BC. He was a murderer and violated the Mosaic Law. He was such a terrible ruler that Caesar Augustus only let him reign for nine years before removing him as ruler of Judea.

Joseph's reservations about Archelaus were correct, and the Lord spoke to Joseph in another dream— his fourth and final dream. The angel of the Lord told Joseph to head towards Galilee back to Nazareth. The small and insignificant town of Nazareth was the original place Mary and Joseph lived when Mary became pregnant with Jesus. Their story began in Nazareth and ended up becoming the location where Jesus was raised.

In Nazareth, Jesus grew up and matured from a child into a man. He had to grow in knowledge and stature like every other child. He grew up in Nazareth with his younger sisters and brothers James, Joseph, Jude, and Simon. He would have learned His earthly father's trade as a carpenter around 10-13 years old. A carpenter was skilled at working with stone, iron, copper, and wood. Carpentry was a middle-class working profession. Carpenters traveled a lot for work, so Jesus likely traveled around the region of Galilee doing laborious outdoor work.

In Nazareth, Jesus matured and grew in wisdom and understanding to begin His earthly ministry to do His heavenly Father's work. Jesus' parents would have raised Him in God's ways. He perfectly obeyed God's Laws— the only person ever to do so. He would have gone to the local synagogue weekly with His family to hear the scriptures being taught on Sabbath. At twelve years of age, Jesus showed great wisdom and understanding of the scriptures when He discussed them at the temple during Passover with the religious leaders.

In Nazareth, Jesus matured and prepared for His ultimate purpose— to share God's truth with people and offer Himself as the perfect, sinless sacrifice to appease God's wrath and provide salvation for those who believe in Him. At about 30 years of age, Jesus began His public ministry and was baptized in the Jordan River by His cousin, John the Baptist. Jesus would grow up to be called a Nazarene, and was the best thing to come from that little town.

Archelaus

Archelaus was one of Herod the Great's sons and became king at just 18 years old. Four days before Herod died, he modified his will to make Archelaus his successor in Judea instead of Herod Antipas. Archelaus was a terrible ruler, just like his father. King Herod died right before Passover in 4 BC. Before Archelaus was officially crowned king by Caesar Augustus, he committed a terrible act in the temple courts the day before Passover. The Jewish people were demanding a change of high priest and wanted Herod's councilors punished. Archelaus felt the people were becoming out of control, so he sent Herodian soldiers into the temple courts and killed 3,000 people the day before Passover— before he was even crowned king. He then canceled Passover for that year. During his short reign, he replaced the high priest position three times for personal profit. The Roman authorities were worried his violent behavior and violation of the Jewish Law would cause a revolt among the Jewish people, so they removed him from his position after nine years.

Galilee

Nazareth was located in the region of Galilee, where Herod Antipas (Archelaus' brother) was governor during Jesus' life. Galilee was the northern part of Israel and was located between the Mediterranean Sea and the Sea of Galilee. It had the highest elevation of Israel, therefore, making it the coolest and wettest part of Israel. Galilee received a lot of rainfall and dew, which helped it be a very fertile land. Galilee was Israel's top producer of wine. Many people were fishermen in this area because of the abundance of fish in the Sea of Galilee and Jordan River. Jesus' first disciples, Peter, Andrew, James, and John were fishermen from Galilee.

Nazareth

Nazareth was a really small village located in the region of Galilee. Nazareth was viewed as an insignificant city, and if you were called a Nazarene it was meant to be an insult. It was located four miles away from Sepphoris, the most robust fortified city in Galilee. It was also located nine miles away from Cana, a key city where Jesus performed His first miracle at a wedding by turning water into wine. Nazareth was a poor village with homes made out of uncut stone, mud, and thatch roofing (straw, branches, or grass).

Family Review

Comprehension Questions:

1. How did Joseph know when it was time to leave Egypt? *The angel of the Lord told him in a dream.*
2. When was Joseph allowed to take his family back to Israel? *After Herod died.*
3. Why didn't Joseph want to live in Judea? *Because Herod's son, Archelaus, was ruler and was just as evil as his father.*
4. Where did Joseph end up settling his family to raise Jesus? *In the small village of Nazareth located in Galilee.*
5. Where were Mary and Joseph living before Jesus was born? *Nazareth*

Application Questions:

1. Joseph and Mary were obedient to the Lord with every aspect of their life. How does their story inspire you to obey the Lord?
2. Is there any command from God that is too small or insignificant to obey?
3. Why does the Lord give us commands to follow?
4. After reading about the birth story of Jesus, what do you think the main focus of Christmas should be? What would you like to do as a family to glorify Jesus this season?

Key Bible Verse:

"And when they had performed everything according to the Law of the Lord, they returned into Galilee, to their own town of Nazareth. And the child grew and became strong, filled with wisdom. And the favor of God was upon him."

Luke 2:39-40

Family Prayer:

Heavenly Father,

Thank you for sharing the details of Jesus' birth story. Thank you for helping us learn more about Jesus' life and helping us realize He was a child and human like us. Thank you for protecting the Savior so we would have salvation. Thank you for this Christmas season and the reminder every year to praise you for sending your Son down to earth to save us. We pray we keep our focus on you and work to grow obedient like Jesus. Help us seek your will and help us fight the temptation to sin. We want more of you and less of ourselves. We love you and thank you for our many blessings. In Jesus' name, Amen.

1. Luke 2 tells us that Joseph and Mary returned to Nazareth after they completed everything according to the Law. Why was it important for Jesus' parents to be Law abiding Jews?

_____

_____

_____

2. Jesus fulfilled the Law perfectly— this included His childhood. How might Jesus' childhood have looked different compared to a child born with sinful nature?

_____

_____

_____

3. Why was it important for Jesus to obey the Law perfectly (completely sinless) from birth to death? Read Hebrews 9:12-10:18. Try reading from the NLT translation for an easier understanding.

_____

_____

_____

4. Matthew said Jesus would be called a Nazarene as spoken by the prophets. Being called a Nazarene was actually an insult and a phrase of contempt. Read the Old Testament prophecies and note how their descriptions could relate to Jesus being called a Nazarene.

Isaiah 53:1-3 _____

_____

Psalm 22:6 _____

_____

5. Read the first two chapters of Matthew and Luke again. Each author shares different details about Jesus' birth. Matthew was writing to a Jewish audience, while Luke was writing to a Gentile audience. Knowing this background, write down what their main focus was in the story and why you think they chose to focus on those particular details.

Matthew 1 & 2: _____

_____

_____

Luke 1 & 2: _____

_____

_____

Reflect

1. Just like Joseph and Mary, the Lord has given each believer specific commands to obey. Read these few verses and write down the specific commands God has given you to obey as a Christian.

Matthew 5:13-16 _____

_____

Matthew 5:44-48 _____

_____

Matthew 22:37-40 _____

_____

Matthew 28:19-20 _____

_____

2. If there is anything we can learn from Mary and Joseph, it is the importance of complete obedience to the Lord. His ways are good and purposeful. How will you intentionally live a life of obedience moving forward, so the Lord is truly King over all aspects of your life?

_____

_____

_____

_____

3. What aspect of God's character do you understand more clearly after reading today's passage? What does this truth of God mean for your walk as a Christian?

_____

_____

_____

_____

Pray

_____

_____

_____

_____

_____

Hymns

Childhood of Jesus
Published in the book of Hymns #115 (1860)

1 In fair green fields of Palestine,

And by its winding rills,

Along the Jordan's sacred stream,

And o'er the vine-clad hills,

2 Once lived and roved the fairest child

That ever blessed the earth;

The holiest, the happiest,

And yet of humblest birth.

3 How beautiful his childhood was,

How fair and undefiled!

Oh, dear to his young mother's heart

Was this pure, sinless child!

4 Kindly in all his deeds and words,

And gentle as the dove;

Obedient, affectionate,

His very soul was love.

Christmas Carol (From Heaven Above to Earth I Come)
Written by Martin Luther (1535)

1 From heaven above to earth I come

To bear good news to every home;

Glad tidings of great joy I bring,

Whereof I now will say and sing:

2 To you this night is born a child

Of Mary, chosen mother mild;

This little child, of lowly birth,

Shall be the joy of all the earth.

3 Give head, my heart, lift up thine eyes!

Who is it in yon manger lies?

Who is this child so young and fair?

The blessed Christ-child lieth there.

4 Ah, dearest Jesus, holy child,

Make thee a bed, soft, undefiled,

Within my heart, that it may be

A quiet chamber, kept for thee.

5 My heart for very joy doth leap,

My lips no more can silence keep;

I too must sing, with joyful tongue,

That sweetest ancient cradle-song:

6 Glory to God in highest heaven,

And unto man sweet peace be given!

While angels sing with pious mirth

A glad New-Year to all the earth.

Source: Hymnary.org

Cinnamon Stick Cross Ornament

Supplies:

- Cinnamon sticks
- Red and white twine
- Hot glue
- Scissors

Directions:

1. Trim your cinnamon sticks so the horizontal stick is slightly shorter than the vertical. My sticks were 2.5" long, so I trimmed the horizontal piece to be 2" long.
2. Glue together and wrap twine around the center. Secure the twine with hot glue.
3. Glue twine to the top of the cinnamon stick to hang.
4. Enjoy these crosses as a fragrant ornament on your tree, or add them as a decoration when you wrap your Christmas gifts. These are a great reminder of who we are celebrating this season!

Craft idea inspired by: CottageChroniclesBlog.com

Cinnamon Apple Cider

Supplies: (Serves 10)

- 12 gala apples, or fuji apples, cored and cubed
- 2 green apples, cored and cubed
- 3 cinnamon sticks
- 1 ginger, thumb sized, peeled
- 2 tsp whole clove
- 1 pinch of kosher salt
- 8 cups water
- ½ cup brown sugar or maple syrup (add more if you want it sweeter)

Directions:

1. Place the cut apples, cinnamon sticks, ginger, cloves, and salt in an 8-quart (7.5-liters) slow cooker. Pour the water over the apples.
2. Cover and cook on high for at least 8 hours or overnight (up to 24 hours).
3. Pour the cider into a separate container using a mesh strainer to separate the solid pieces. Press as much liquid out of the apples with a spoon against the strainer.
4. Whisk in the brown sugar or syrup until dissolved. Serve hot or store in the refrigerator in a covered container to serve later. Reheat before serving.

AYALON VALLEY
(NORTH OF JERUSALEM)

APPENDIX

EXTRAS & RESOURCES

And the Word became flesh and dwelt

among us, and we have seen his glory,

glory as of the only Son from the Father, full

of grace and truth.

JOHN 1:14 ESV

Make a copy of this page to cut out for your Bethlehem ornament in Lesson 2.
You can also print out your own copy from Hymnary.org.

O Little Town of Bethlehem

1 O lit-tle town of Beth-le-hem, how still we__ see thee lie!
2 For Christ is born of Ma - ry, and ga thered all a - bove,
3 How si-lent-ly, how si-lent-ly the won drous gift is given!
4 O ho - ly Child of Beth-le- hem, des-cend to__ us, we pray;

A - bove thy deep and dream-less sleep the si - lent_stars go
while mor-tals sleep, the an - gels keep their watch of__ won dering
So God im-parts to hu - man hearts the bles sings of his
cast out our sin, and en - ter in; be born in__ us to -

by. Yet in thy dark streets shin - eth the e - ver - las-ting
love, O mor-ning stars, to - ge - ther pro-claim the ho - ly
heaven. No ear may hear his co - ming, but in this world of
day. We hear the Christ-mas an - gels the great glad ti-dings

Light; the hopes and fears of
birth, and prai - ses sing to
sin, where meek souls will re -
tell; O come to us, a -

all the years are met in thee to - night.
God the King, and peace to all on earth.
ceive him still, the dear Christ en - ters in.
bide with us, our Lord Em - ma - nu - el.

Hymnary.org

Holy Land Map

Reference this map as you study the lessons to help visualize where Joseph and Mary traveled.

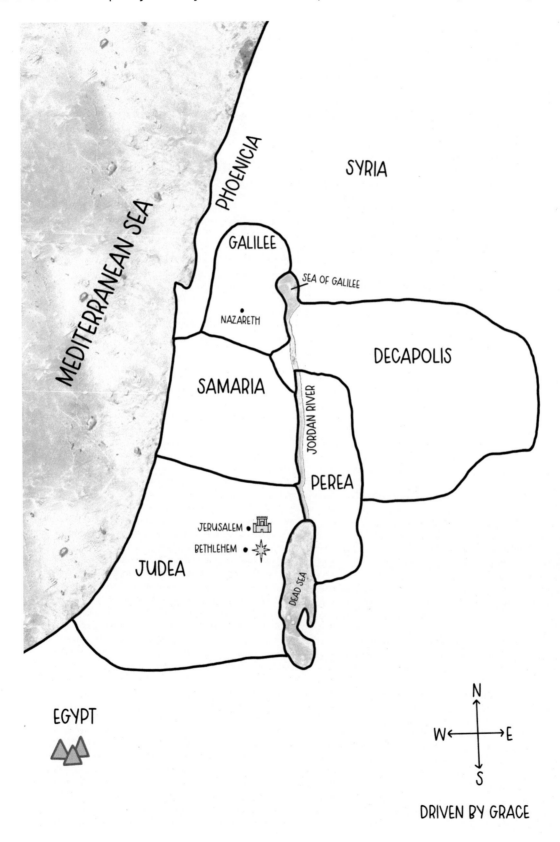

Lesson 1:

- Guzik, D. (2018). *Luke 1 Commentary*. Enduring Word. Retrieved September 12, 2022, from https://enduringword.com/bible-commentary/luke-1/
- Hopler, W. (2021). *How Old Was Mary When She Had Jesus?* CrossWalk.com. Retrieved September 12, 2022, from https://www.crosswalk.com/faith/bible-study/how-old-was-mary-when-she-had-jesus.html
- *How old was Mary when Jesus was born?* (n.d.). GotQuestions.org. Retrieved September 12, 2022, from https://www.gotquestions.org/how-old-was-Mary.html
- Keener, C. S. (2014). *The IVP Bible background commentary: New Testament (pp.178-182)*. Intervarsity Press.
- Koiter, I. W. K. (2016). Nazareth. In J. D. Barry, D. Bomar, D. R. Brown, R. Klippenstein, D. Mangum, C. Sinclair Wolcott, L. Wentz, E. Ritzema, & W. Widder (Eds.), The Lexham Bible Dictionary. Lexham Press.
- *What does the Bible say about the angel Gabriel?* (n.d.). GotQuestions.org. Retrieved September 12, 2022, from https://www.gotquestions.org/angel-Gabriel.html
- Zacharias, H. D. (2016). Gabriel the Archangel. In J. D. Barry, D. Bomar, D. R. Brown, R. Klippenstein, D. Mangum, C. Sinclair Wolcott, L. Wentz, E. Ritzema, & W. Widder (Eds.), The Lexham Bible Dictionary. Lexham Press.

Lesson 2:

- Hershey, D. (2019). *What Bethlehem Means to Israel in the Bible and Today*. FirmIsrael.org. Retrieved September 12, 2022, from https://firmisrael.org/learn/what-bethlehem-means-to-israel-in-bible-and-today/
- Keener, C. S. (2014). *The IVP Bible background commentary: New Testament (pp. 48)*. Intervarsity Press.
- Mangum, D. (2016). Bethlehem of Judah. In J. D. Barry, D. Bomar, D. R. Brown, R. Klippenstein, D. Mangum, C. Sinclair Wolcott, L. Wentz, E. Ritzema, & W. Widder (Eds.), The Lexham Bible Dictionary. Lexham Press.
- *What is the importance of Bethlehem in the Bible?* (n.d.). GotQuestions.org. Retrieved September 12, 2022, from https://www.gotquestions.org/Bethlehem-in-the-Bible.html

Lesson 3:

- Buck, Tim. (2021) *Migdal Edar, The True Story Behind The Birthplace of Jesus*. Focus On The End Times Ministry (fotet.org). Retrieved September 14, 2022, from https://fotet.org/migdal-edar-the-true-story-behind-the-birthplace-of-jesus/
- Eder, Tower of. (2016). In J. D. Barry, D. Bomar, D. R. Brown, R. Klippenstein, D. Mangum, C. Sinclair Wolcott, L. Wentz, E. Ritzema, & W. Widder (Eds.), The Lexham Bible Dictionary. Lexham Press.
- Guzik, D. (2018). Luke 2 Commentary. Enduring Word. Retrieved September 12, 2022, from https://enduringword.com/bible-commentary/luke-2/
- Montonini, M. (2016). Shepherd. In J. D. Barry, D. Bomar, D. R. Brown, R. Klippenstein, D. Mangum, C. Sinclair Wolcott, L. Wentz, E. Ritzema, & W. Widder (Eds.), The Lexham Bible Dictionary. Lexham Press.
- Pack, H. R. & Smith, D. (2020). Who Were the Shepherds. Redeemer of Israel. Retrieved September 12, 2022, from http://www.redeemerofisrael.org/2020/12/who-were-shepherds.html
- What does it mean that Jesus is the Savior? (n.d.). GotQuestions.org. Retrieved September 14, 2022, from https://www.gotquestions.org/Jesus-is-the-Savior.html
- *What was a shepherd in the Bible?* (n.d.). GotQuestions.org. Retrieved September 14, 2022, from https://www.gotquestions.org/shepherd-in-the-Bible.html
- Wight, F. (1953). Manners and customs of Bible lands. Moody Press. Retrieved September 14, 2022, from https://www.ancient-hebrew.org/manners/shepherd-life-the-care-of-sheep-and-goats.htm

Lesson 4:

- Anna the Prophetess. (2016). In J. D. Barry, D. Bomar, D. R. Brown, R. Klippenstein, D. Mangum, C. Sinclair Wolcott, L. Wentz, E. Ritzema, & W. Widder (Eds.), The Lexham Bible Dictionary. Lexham Press.

- Britannica (n.d.). Jerusalem Administration and Society. Retrieved September 12, 2022, from https://www.britannica.com/place/Jerusalem/Administration-and-society
- Rodrigo, D. (n.d.). English: A view of Jerusalem (Israel). Wikimedia Commons. Retrieved September 14, 2022, from https://commons.wikimedia.org/wiki/File:A_view_of_Jerusalem_(Israel).jpg [Public Domain]
- Shepherd, C. E. (2016). Jerusalem. In J. D. Barry, D. Bomar, D. R. Brown, R. Klippenstein, D. Mangum, C. Sinclair Wolcott, L. Wentz, E. Ritzema, & W. Widder (Eds.), The Lexham Bible Dictionary. Lexham Press.
- Strauss, M. L. (2016). Messiah. In J. D. Barry, D. Bomar, D. R. Brown, R. Klippenstein, D. Mangum, C. Sinclair Wolcott, L. Wentz, E. Ritzema, & W. Widder (Eds.), The Lexham Bible Dictionary. Lexham Press.
- *Who was Anna the prophetess in the Bible?* (n.d.). GotQuestions.org. Retrieved September 14, 2022, from https://www.gotquestions.org/Anna-the-prophetess.html
- *Who was Simeon in the Bible?* (n.d.). GotQuestions.org. Retrieved September 14, 2022, from https://www.gotquestions.org/Simeon-in-the-Bible.html

Lesson 5:

- Bibles, C. (2008). ESV Study Bible: English Standard Version (Matthew 2). Crossway Bibles.
- Dexter, J. (n.d.) *Matthew 1 Inductive Bible Study.* StudyandObey.com. Retrieved September 12, 2022, from https://studyandobey.com/inductive-bible-study/matthew-studies/matthew-1/
- Guzik, D. (2018). Matthew 2 Commentary. Enduring Word. Retrieved September 12, 2022, from https://enduringword.com/bible-commentary/matthew-2/
- Keener, C. S. (2014). The IVP Bible background commentary: New Testament (pp.47-51). Intervarsity Press.studyandobey.com/journey-of-the-wise-men/
- Krause, M. (2016). Wise Men, Magi. In J. D. Barry, D. Bomar, D. R. Brown, R. Klippenstein, D. Mangum, C. Sinclair Wolcott, L. Wentz, E. Ritzema, & W. Widder (Eds.), The Lexham Bible Dictionary. Lexham Press.
- *Why did the Magi bring gold, frankincense, and myrrh to Jesus?* (2010). GotQuestions.org. Retrieved September 12, 2022, from https://www.gotquestions.org/gold-frankincense-myrrh.html
- Who was Herod the Great? (n.d.). GotQuestions.org. Retrieved September 14, 2022, from https://www.gotquestions.org/Herod-the-Great.html
- Wikipedia Contributors. (2019, July 18). Herod the Great. Wikipedia; Wikimedia Foundation. Retrieved September 12, 2022, from https://en.wikipedia.org/wiki/Herod_the_Great

Lesson 6:

- Barry, J. D., Mangum, D., Brown, D. R., Heiser, M. S., Custis, M., Ritzema, E., Whitehead, M. M., Grigoni, M. R., & Bomar, D. (2012, 2016). Faithlife Study Bible (Mt 2:13). Lexham Press.
- Dexter, J. (n.d.) *Matthew 2 Inductive Bible Study.* StudyandObey.com. Retrieved September 12, 2022, fromhttps://studyandobey.com/inductive-bible-study/matthew-2/
- Guzik, D. (2018). Matthew 2 Commentary. Enduring Word. Retrieved September 12, 2022, from https://enduringword.com/bible-commentary/matthew-2/
- Herod the Great. (n.d.). Wikipedia. Retrieved September 12, 2022 from https://en.wikipedia.org/wiki/Herod_the_Great#Architectural_achievements
- *Herod the Great.* (n.d). Wikipedia. Retrieved September 12, 2022, from https://en.wikipedia.org/wiki/Herod_the_Great#Death
- Team, B. M. C. (2019, September 18). *Jews in Ancient Egypt.* Pearl of Great Price Central. Retrieved September 12, 2022, from https://pearlofgreatpricecentral.org/jews-in-ancient-egypt/

Lesson 7:

- Easton, M. G. (1893). In Illustrated Bible Dictionary and Treasury of Biblical History, Biography, Geography, Doctrine, and Literature (p. 128). Harper & Brothers.
- Gottheil, R. & Ginzbery, L. (n.d.) *Archelaus*. JewishEncyclopedia.com. Retrieved September 12, 2022, from https://www.jewishencyclopedia.com/articles/1729-archelaus
- Koiter, I. W. K. (2016). Nazareth. In J. D. Barry, D. Bomar, D. R. Brown, R. Klippenstein, D. Mangum, C. Sinclair Wolcott, L. Wentz, E. Ritzema, & W. Widder (Eds.), The Lexham Bible Dictionary. Lexham Press.
- Laney, J. C. (2016). Galilee. In J. D. Barry, D. Bomar, D. R. Brown, R. Klippenstein, D. Mangum, C. Sinclair Wolcott, L. Wentz, E. Ritzema, & W. Widder (Eds.), The Lexham Bible Dictionary. Lexham Press.
- McDowell, S. (2022). *What was it like for Jesus to be a Carpenter?* SeanMcdowell.org. Retrieved September 12, 2022, from https://seanmcdowell.org/blog/what-it-was-like-for-jesus-to-be-a-carpenter
- Wikipedia Contributors. (2019, August 10). Herod Archelaus. Wikipedia; Wikimedia Foundation. Retrieved September 12, 2022, from https://en.wikipedia.org/wiki/Herod_Archelaus

Sources used for all lessons:

- Hamilton, A. (2021). The journey: Walking the Road to Bethlehem. Abingdon Press.
- Holy Bible English Standard Version Study Bible. (2014). Crossway Books.
- Images for lessons 1-3 and 5-7 are from Canva Pro database.
- Macarthur, J. (2010). The MacArthur Study Bible: New American Standard Bible. Nashville, Tennessee: Thomas Nelson.

Other Resources

Easter Studies

Adult & children's Bible studies for the death & resurrection of Jesus.

66 Bible Verse Journal

Adults and children can memorize a theme verse from each book of the Bible with these memory journals.

Exodus Bible Study

Study the birth of Moses through the 10 commandments with Exodus studies part 1 & 2.

Motherhood Study

Motherhood lessons from 5 key biblical women: Proverbs 31, Eve, Sarah, Hannah & Mary.

Check out more resources at DrivenByGrace.com

Thank you!

Let's Connect!

 @DrivenByGrace

Contact

Lindsey@DrivenByGrace.com

Share

#DrivenByGrace

Shop

www.DrivenByGrace.com

Made in the USA
Columbia, SC
21 October 2022